Businesses

Jenny and Tasmin Simmonds run a marketing agency, Creative+, specialising in the design of holiday brochures and websites for tour companies.

F 1 What is the purpose of a business? **(1 mark)**

Select **one** answer.

The purpose of a business is to produce goods and services:

A ☐ for the government

B ☑ to meet the needs of customers

C ☐ to meet the needs of suppliers

D ☐ and maximise profit

F 2 Which **one** of the following is **most** likely to be a customer for Creative+? **(1 mark)**

> Guided >

Select **one** answer.

A ☑ The public sector

B ☐ The general public

~~C ☐ A business supplying paper to Creative+~~

D ☐ A business selling adventure holidays in Africa

> It isn't option C because the business is a **supplier** not a **customer**.

E 3 Which of the following **two** things might Jenny and Tasmin have considered when setting up Creative+? **(2 marks)**

Select **two** answers.

A ☑ How the business will be financed

B ☐ The demand for oil in the economy ✗

C ☐ The level of government spending in the economy ✗

D ☑ What legal aspects have to be considered

E ☐ Global weather patterns ✗

Understanding customer needs 1

Samit Singh works as a bus driver for a local transport company in Stratford-upon-Avon. He is keen to start his own business providing an express bus service between Stratford-upon-Avon and Birmingham Airport. He spent a week doing market research. Samit interviewed 200 airport users in Stratford-upon-Avon town centre and some of the results are shown below.

Figure 1: Age profile of people who would use the service

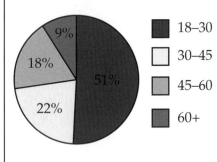

- 18–30
- 30–45
- 45–60
- 60+

51%
22%
18%
9%

Table 1: The proportion of people interviewed prepared to pay different fares

Return fare	% of people prepared to pay
£14–£16	94%
£16–£18	76%
£18–£20	59%
£20–£24	31%
£24–£28	12%
£28+	3%

 C

1   Study Figure 1 and Table 1. According to this information, which **three** conclusions can Samit draw from the data? **(3 marks)**

 Guided

 EXAM ALERT

Select **three** answers.

> Students have struggled with exam questions similar to this – **be prepared!** ResultsPlus

A   ☑ Only a minority of elderly customers would use the service

B   ☐ Only six people of those interviewed would pay more than £28 for the service

C   ☑ The 18–30 age group is the largest market segment

D   ☑ The best price to charge would be £15

> It isn't option F because profit cannot be determined without cost and sales data.

E   ☐ It is not worth trying to market the service to the over 45s

F   ☐ ~~The business could make a profit only if £19 was charged for the service~~

 F

2   Which of the following is **not** likely to be a customer need? **(1 mark)**

Select **one** answer.

A   ☑ Good cash flow

B   ☐ A fair price

C   ☐ Good quality

D   ☐ Good customer service

REVISE EDEXCEL GCSE

Business

Units 1, 3 and 5

REVISION WORKBOOK

Series Consultant: Harry Smith

Authors: Rob Jones and Andrew Redfern

A note from the publisher

In order to ensure that this resource offers high-quality support for the associated Edexcel qualification, it has been through a review process by the awarding body to confirm that it fully covers the teaching and learning content of the specification or part of a specification at which it is aimed, and demonstrates an appropriate balance between the development of subject skills, knowledge and understanding, in addition to preparation for assessment.

While the publishers have made every attempt to ensure that advice on the qualification and its assessment is accurate, the official specification and associated assessment guidance materials are the only authoritative source of information and should always be referred to for definitive guidance.

Edexcel examiners have not contributed to any sections in this resource relevant to examination papers for which they have responsibility.

No material from an endorsed resource will be used verbatim in any assessment set by Edexcel.

Endorsement of a resource does not mean that the resource is required to achieve this Edexcel qualification, nor does it mean that it is the only suitable material available to support the qualification, and any resource lists produced by the awarding body shall include this and other appropriate resources.

ALWAYS LEARNING

PEARSON

Contents

This book covers the GCSE Business Studies, and GCSE Business Studies and Economics pathways. If you are studying:

GCSE Business Studies - you should work through Unit 1 and Unit 3

GCSE Business Studies and Economics – you should work through Unit 1 and Unit 5

GCSE Business Studies (short course) – you should work through Unit 1.

A small bit of small print

Edexcel publishes Sample Assessment Material and the Specification on its website. This is the official content and this book should be used in conjunction with it. The questions in this book have been written to help you practise what you have learned in your revision. Remember: the real exam questions may not look like this.

Target grades

Target grades are quoted in this book for some of the questions. Students targeting this grade should be aiming to get most of the marks available. Students targeting a higher grade should be aiming to get all of the marks available.

A grade allocated to a question represents the highest grade covered by that question. Sub-parts of the question may cover lower grade material.

Understanding customer needs 2

Jeremy Nolan runs Nolan's, a car service centre in Leeds. In the last three years his profit has fallen from £98 000 to £12 000. He is thinking of doing some primary market research to find out possible reasons for this. His aim is to collect some qualitative data from customers.

G 1 Which of the following is **not** an example of primary market research for Jeremy? **(1 mark)**

Select **one** answer.

A ☐ Conducting a telephone survey of past customers

B ☐ Asking existing customers to complete a feedback questionnaire

C ☐ Setting up a customer suggestion box in the reception area

D ☑ Searching the internet to find out the prices charged by competitors

D 2 Which of the following is an example of qualitative data for Jeremy? **(1 mark)**

Guided

Select **one** answer.

A ☐ The number of car owners within a 5-mile radius of Nolan's

B ☑ Information about the views of customers

C ☐ ~~The percentage decline in market share in recent years~~

D ☐ The current value of market share

> It isn't option C because this is **quantitative** data.

D 3 Which **two** of the following are advantages of primary market research? **(2 marks)**

Select **two** answers.

A ☐ It is very cheap

B ☐ It is less time-consuming than secondary research

C ☑ It is more specific to the needs of a business

D ☑ It is more up to date

E ☐ It can be done only by market-research agencies

Market mapping

Mario Tevez wants to open a restaurant specialising in South American cuisine. He thinks there might be a gap in the market in his home town of Odmoor in Yorkshire. He has drawn up a market map to identify whether there are any gaps in the market. There are currently eight restaurants in Odmoor.

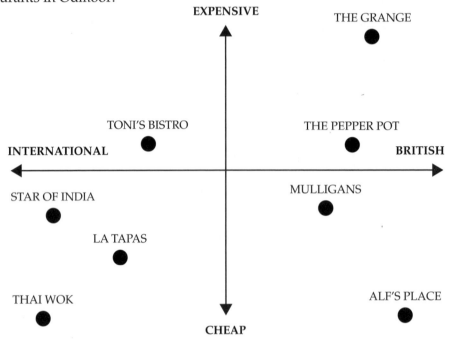

F

1 According to the market map, where is there a business gap in the market?   **(1 mark)**

Select **one** answer.

A business that provides:

A ☐ cheap international food

B ☐ cheap British food

C ☑ expensive international food

D ☐ expensive British food

C

2 Which **two** of the following are benefits to Mario from segmenting the market?   **(2 marks)**

Select **two** answers.

Segmenting the market will help to:

A ☑ differentiate the product

B ☐ improve internal communication in the business

C ☐ reduce start-up costs

D ☐ reduce staff turnover

E ☑ focus on a specific customer group

Competition

> Valerie and Norman Trembath own a dairy farm in Cornwall. In 2007 they decided to use some of the milk they produced to make their own brand of ice cream. After analysing the local competition they developed a brand called 'Truro's Best'. It is very rich and creamy, and it is sold at a premium price. Most of their customers are in the catering industry – hotels and restaurants. Valerie and Norman now have an established product range and also produce ice cream in any flavour to order.

C

1 Which **two** of the following suggest that there was an opportunity in the local market for Valerie and Norman Trembath's ice cream?   **(2 marks)**

Select **two** answers.

A ☐ Unemployment in the region was rising

B ☐ Ice cream is made from milk

C ☐ There was only one supplier of premium-priced ice cream in the area

D ☐ The pound is getting stronger against the euro

E ☐ Large ice-cream manufacturers could not supply unique ice-cream flavours to order

D

2 In what way have Valerie and Norman differentiated their ice cream?   **(1 mark)**

> **Guided**

Select **one** answer.

A ☐ ~~They target the catering industry~~

B ☐ They can produce any flavour ice cream to order

C ☐ They supply the local market

D ☐ Their cost base is low

> It isn't option A because targeting a specific market does not mean that they are making their product different from those of their competitors.

D

3 Valerie and Norman have an established product range. This means that: **(1 mark)**

Select **one** answer.

A ☐ they make and sell a group of similar products

B ☐ all their products are the same

C ☐ all their products are home-made

D ☐ they could export their ice cream in the future

Added value 1

Amy Wong is a party organiser. Her business – Parties Ltd – organises a wide range of parties for weddings, birthdays, anniversaries, office parties, Christmas and other social events in the Cheltenham area. The company finds party locations and organises catering, music, decoration, drinks, costumes, transport and any other service that is required by the client.

C 1 Which of the following best describes **added value** in a business?   **(1 mark)**

Select **one** answer.

A ☐ Price – total cost

B ☐ The difference between what a business pays its suppliers and what it receives for selling its products.

C ☐ Variable costs – price

D ☐ The difference between what a business pays its employees and what it receives for selling its products

D 2 Amy charged a client £12 500 for an office party that she organised. Total variable costs for the event came to £5400. What is the added value?   **(1 mark)**

Select **one** answer.

A ☐ £12 500

B ☐ £17 900

C ☐ £5400

D ☐ £7100

D 3 Which of the following might be a way that Amy could add value in her business?   **(1 mark)**

Select **one** answer.

A ☐ Charging a premium price

B ☐ Lowering average costs

C ☐ Relocating the business to London

D ☐ Providing clients with a convenient service

> Added value is the thing that customers would be willing to pay more for.

Added value 2

> Ellie Harrison owns the Witney Flower Shop, located in the high street in Witney, Oxfordshire. The business is established and successful. Ellie believes the success is the result of her unique selling point: Ellie imports exotic flowers such as orchids for her customers. No other flower shop in the area provides this service.

C

1 Which **two** of the following are strategies that Ellie might use to help her business achieve high levels of added value? **(2 marks)**

> Guided

Select **two** answers.

A ☐ ~~Operate with a 25% mark-up~~

B ☐ Offer a free delivery service (within a 5-mile radius)

C ☐ Ask customers to provide feedback

D ☐ Produce accurate cash-flow forecasts

E ☐ Offer an online ordering and messaging service

> It isn't option A because operating with a set mark-up does not provide any **added value** for the customer.

C

2 Why is added value important for a business such as the Witney Flower Shop? **(1 mark)**

Select **one** answer.

A ☐ It helps to lower staff turnover

B ☐ Higher added value raises staff morale

C ☐ It helps to lower profit margins

D ☐ The higher the added value, the sooner costs can be met and the quicker the business will make a profit

D

3 The Witney Flower Shop is the only flower shop in the area that imports exotic flowers for customers.

Which of the following best defines the term 'unique selling point'? **(1 mark)**

Select **one** answer.

A ☐ A location where no competitors operate

B ☐ A feature that makes the product attractive to consumers

C ☐ A characteristic that makes it different from those of competitors

D ☐ A reason for buying a product

Franchising 1

Sweeny Dog is a franchise operation providing pet services such as dog walking, pet grooming and pet care for absent pet-owners. Sandie Robinson is an animal lover, and she also wants to start her own business. However, she does not want to take too much risk. She is considering taking out a franchise with Sweeny Dog, which costs £9995.

(D) 1   Which of the following is the franchisee in this case?   **(1 mark)**

Select **one** answer.

A ☐ The government

B ☐ Sandie Robinson

C ☐ Sweeny Dog

D ☐ Pet owners

(D) 2   Which of the following is **not** a feature of the Sweeny Dog franchise?   **(1 mark)**

Select **one** answer.

A ☐ An initial fee is paid by the franchisee to the franchisor

B ☐ The franchisee can operate anywhere in the country

C ☐ The franchisor provides the franchisee with guidance and advice

D ☐ Buying a franchise reduces the risk when setting up a business

(D) 3   Which **two** of the following are benefits to Sandie Robinson of buying a Sweeny Dog franchise?   **(2 marks)**

> **Guided**

Select **two** answers.

A ☐ ~~Sandie will pay a lower rate of income tax on any profit made by the business~~

B ☐ Sweeny Dog will provide guidance and advice to Sandie

C ☐ Sandie will have to register as a public limited company

D ☐ Sandie will operate in an exclusive area

E ☐ Sweeny Dog will provide Sandie with start-up capital

> It isn't option A because Sandie would pay the same rate of income tax if she were to set up a business without a franchise.

Franchising 2

Adam Lewandowski works as an environmental officer for a large property company. He is thinking of buying a franchise. He has identified a franchisor called Ecoliving, which was established in 2004. It is a distributor of innovative and sustainable heating, cooling and ventilation systems. For an initial fee of £24 950, Ecoliving offers franchisees the following:

- a three-month induction programme and ongoing training certification
- initial display stock of product and equipment
- deposit on a vehicle and vehicle livery
- branded clothing
- manuals
- launch advertising
- in-field support, and more.

1 Which **three** of the following are benefits to Adam of buying an Ecoliving franchise rather than operating as a sole trader?   **(3 marks)**

> Guided

Select **three** answers.

A ☐ Ecoliving is an established brand

B ☐ Franchises do not have to comply with employment legislation

~~C ☐ Ecoliving provides free access to accountants and solicitors~~

D ☐ Franchisees do not have to pay interest on business loans

E ☐ Ecoliving provides continued help and support

F ☐ There is a higher chance of survival

> It isn't option C because the case study doesn't suggest that Ecoliving provides free access to accountants and solicitors.

2 Which **two** of the following are possible drawbacks to Adam of buying an Ecoliving franchise?   **(2 marks)**

Select **two** answers.

EXAM ALERT

A ☐ Adam will have a lack of freedom when making business decisions

B ☐ The £24 950 set-up fee is quite high

C ☐ Adam will not be permitted to sell the business

D ☐ Franchisees have to pay tax on behalf of the franchisor

E ☐ Adam will need to pass environmental exams before buying the franchise

> Students have struggled with exam questions similar to this – **be prepared!** ResultsPlus

> Make sure you read the case study carefully so you understand the **context** of the business.

Enterprise

G 1 Which **one** of the following best defines the role of an entrepreneur?   **(1 mark)**

Select **one** answer.

An entrepreneur is a person who:

A ☐ enjoys working in the service sector

B ☐ wants to avoid paying income tax

C ☐ owns and runs their own business and takes risks

D ☐ runs a business while the owner is away on holiday

F 2 Which **two** of the following are characteristics of an entrepreneur?   **(2 marks)**

> **Guided**

Select **two** answers.

A ☐ A willingness to undertake a new venture

B ☐ A very wealthy family background

C ☐ A preparedness to take risks

D ☐ Not willing to take financial risks

E ☐ An education at least up to A-level

> It isn't option E because people do not need academic qualifications to be an entrepreneur.

E 3 Businesses provide goods and services.

Which **three** of the following are examples of goods?   **(3 marks)**

Select **three** answers.

A ☐ A component for a car engine

B ☐ A restaurant meal

C ☐ A taxi ride

D ☐ Dental treatment

E ☐ A packet of crisps

F ☐ A pair of denim jeans

Thinking creatively

Ethan Grant went to an agricultural college in order to qualify as a farm manager. When studying he became very interested in the damage caused by pigeons to crops. Pigeons attack crops such as broccoli, cabbages and cauliflower. They peck at the leaves and rip off portions, often leaving just the stalks. The damage can be severe, resulting in lower yields and lost revenue for farmers. Ethan decided that with some creative thinking he would try to devise a method of preventing this damage, and he set up a business based on his idea.

B

1 Ethan began his creative thinking by adopting a blue-skies thinking approach to the problem.

> **Guided**

Which **one** of the following best describes blue-skies thinking?   **(1 mark)**

Select **one** answer.

It is a technique where the participants:

A ☐ use a quantitative approach to problem solving

B ☐ make the most of available technology when solving a problem

C ☐ are encouraged to think of as many ideas as possible about a problem

D ☐ solve problems using dice

> It isn't option D because the use of dice will not help to solve problems.

C

2 Ethan has heard that lateral thinking will help him come up with new ideas.

What is lateral thinking?   **(1 mark)**

Select **one** answer.

A ☐ A group approach to generating ideas

B ☐ Thinking differently to try to find new and unexpected ideas (sometimes called 'thinking outside the box')

C ☐ A quantitative approach to generating ideas

D ☐ A technique where the participants are encouraged to think of as many ideas as possible about a problem

C

3 Which **two** of the following might be benefits to Ethan of creative thinking?   **(2 marks)**

Select **two** answers.

A ☐ Avoids the need for lateral thinking

B ☐ He might develop a unique idea to solve the problem

C ☐ Avoids the need to write a business plan

D ☐ He might gain a competitive edge in the market

E ☐ Easier to raise finance when starting a business

Questions entrepreneurs ask

> Sarah Binny is a retired primary school teacher. She wants to set up a business producing electronic learning materials for young children to use at home before they begin school. She thinks that simple picture-based computer games can be designed to help youngsters with basic arithmetic, word recognition and a foreign language.

D　**1** Which **two** of the following might be reasons for asking questions when Sarah starts her business? **(2 marks)**

Select **two** answers.

　A　☐　Helps to identify potential problems and pitfalls

　B　☐　She will not have to raise capital for the business

　C　☐　Improves the cash flow of the business in early trading

　D　☐　Eliminates the need for marketing

　E　☐　Helps to clarify objectives for the business

F　**2** Which **one** of the following questions relating to the purpose and direction of the business is likely to be asked by Sarah when setting up? **(1 mark)**

Guided

Select **one** answer.

　A　☐　~~How much tax will I pay on my business profit?~~

　B　☐　Where can I buy business stationery?

　C　☐　Why do I want to start my own business?

　D　☐　Will I need a licence to set up a business?

> It isn't option A because it does not relate to the **purpose** and **direction** of Sarah's business.

D　**3** Sarah thought it would be helpful to ask a number of 'what if' questions when setting up her business.

What is the purpose of 'what if' questions? **(1 mark)**

Select **one** answer.

　A　☐　They allow an entrepreneur to assess the value and likelihood of any possible outcome

　B　☐　They ensure that the business cannot fail

　C　☐　They help to recruit staff from overseas

　D　☐　They allow an entrepreneur to make a profit

Invention and innovation

While working for a creative-software company, Sonia Trent had an idea for a new mobile phone app. The app, which she proposed to call 'Trip Planner', would search the internet and come up with the cheapest way to travel between two different destinations – nationally and internationally. It would look at all types of transport and link them together if a particular journey required, say, a taxi, a train, a flight and a bus. The app needed further development and Sonia hoped to build in an automatic booking and payment system as well.

E

1 Business ideas come from many different sources. In this case Sonia's idea was related to her work.

Which **one** of the following is **not** a source for a business idea?   **(1 mark)**

Select **one** answer.

A ☐ Research and development

B ☐ Finding a weakness in an existing product through experience

C ☐ Copying or adapting existing products

D ☐ Taking a Degree in Business Studies

D

2 Which **one** of the following **best** defines the term 'invention'?   **(1 mark)**

⟩ Guided ⟩

Select **one** answer.

A ☐ Launching a product in a niche market

B ☐ The process of transforming new ideas into products that can be marketed

C ☐ The discovery of new processes and potential new products, typically after a period of research

D̶ ̶☐̶ ̶C̶o̶p̶y̶i̶n̶g̶ ̶o̶r̶ ̶a̶d̶a̶p̶t̶i̶n̶g̶ ̶a̶n̶ ̶e̶x̶i̶s̶t̶i̶n̶g̶ ̶p̶r̶o̶d̶u̶c̶t̶

EXAM ALERT

Students have struggled with exam questions similar to this – **be prepared!** ResultsPlus

It isn't option D because this describes an **adaptation**.

F

3 Sonia thought it might be necessary to protect her new mobile phone app.

Which **two** of the following are methods of protection for a new business idea?   **(2 marks)**

Select **two** answers.

A ☐ Business plan

B ☐ Contract of employment

C ☐ Patent

D ☐ Copyright

E ☐ Innovation

Taking a calculated risk

Marcus Rampaul works for the Metropolitan Police Force. He wants to set up an advisory security service to businesses in South London. Using his experience of crime against businesses, he plans to sell advice to help businesses protect against crime and save money. Marcus reckons his chances of success are quite high, at 80%. He also thinks that he could make about £50 000 profit per annum once the business is established. However, the initial research, marketing and setting-up costs would amount to £15 000. The risk of failure is only 20%, but he would lose money and sacrifice a good job paying £32 000 a year. In March 2012, he left his job and started his business.

C

1 Marcus is taking a calculated risk in setting up his business.

What is meant by a 'calculated risk'? **(1 mark)**

Select **one** answer.

A ☐ The probability of a negative event occurring

B ☐ The probability of a positive event occurring

C ☐ The probability that the business will succeed

D ☐ A quantitative approach to business planning

C

2 Which **one** of the following would be an example of a calculated risk for Marcus's business? **(1 mark)**

Select **one** answer.

A ☐ 90% of Marcus's customers will be in South London

B ☐ If the business succeeds it will make £50 000 profit a year

C ☐ If the business fails Marcus will lose £15 000

D ☐ There is a 20% chance that Marcus's business will fail

C

3 Which **two** of the following are disadvantages for Marcus's business? **(2 marks)**

> Guided >

Select **two** answers.

A ☐ There is an 80% chance that the business will be successful

B ☐ There could be many competitors selling security advice

C ☐ The £15 000 set-up costs are quite low

D ☐ Marcus has valuable experience in security and crime against business

> It isn't option D because this describes an **upside**.

E ☐ Businesses generally will not be interested in protecting themselves against crime because they think it will be a waste of money

Other important enterprise skills

Janice Potts is a fanatical supporter of Aston Villa. She currently works in the ticket office at Villa Park but wants to set up her own business in the football industry. She is very friendly with a number of the apprentice footballers and has helped them get settled when they leave home to join the club. Janice thinks that she could offer football clubs a range of services – for example, finding suitable accommodation for young players, and organising advisory and educational services such as financial planning, media skills, English language and communication skills. This would help young footballers settle more quickly into their new environment.

F

1   Janice might improve her chances of success if she can make connections between ideas. What is the diagram called that records words and ideas that are connected to a central word or idea?   **(1 mark)**

Select **one** answer.

A ☐ Market map

B ☐ Mindmap

C ☐ Product life cycle

D ☐ Boston Matrix

D

2   Janice will need a range of enterprise skills if she is to be successful. Which **two** of the following are **not** enterprise skills?   **(2 marks)**

⟩ **Guided** ⟩

Select **two** answers.

A ☐ Thinking ahead

B̶ ̶☐̶ ̶E̶f̶f̶e̶c̶t̶i̶v̶e̶ ̶p̶l̶a̶n̶n̶i̶n̶g̶

C ☐ Having a large personal wealth

D ☐ Seeing opportunities

E ☐ Health-and-safety awareness

> It isn't option B because effective planning is a very important enterprise skill.

E

3   Which **one** of the following would Janice need to help overcome the inevitable setbacks when running her business?   **(1 mark)**

Select **one** answer

A ☐ A bank loan

B ☐ Drive and determination

C ☐ An accountant

D ☐ Effective planning

Objectives when starting up

> Theresa O'Neil had worked for a large supermarket chain for eight years and by the age of 24, she wanted to run her own retail business. She was creative, driven and wanted to be her own boss. Her father lent Theresa £40000, plus she used £10000 of her savings to open a shop. The store, located in the Scottish town of Fort William near Ben Nevis, sold outdoor pursuit equipment and accessories. Her initial aim was to ensure that the business was still trading in two years' time.

(F)

1 Which **one** of the following was Theresa's first business objective?   **(1 mark)**

Select **one** answer

A ☐ Profit maximisation

B ☐ Survival

C ☐ Growth

D ☐ Market domination

(C)

2 Which **one** of the following was a non-financial objective for Theresa's business?   **(1 mark)**

> Guided

Select **one** answer

A ☐ Revenue maximisation

B ☐ Independence

C ☐ Profit maximisation

~~D ☐ Generation of private wealth.~~

> It isn't option D because generating private wealth is a financial objective.

(C)

3 Sometimes businesses are set up to help others.

Which **one** of the following would be an example of this?   **(1 mark)**

Select **one** answer

A ☐ Charity

B ☐ Multinational corporation

C ☐ Sole trader

D ☐ Co-operative

Qualities shown by entrepreneurs

Nurse Kim Hurst was made redundant from a local hospital in 2010 as a result of government cuts. She received a £23 000 redundancy payment and decided to set up a business providing home care for the elderly. Kim was determined to make the business succeed but knew there was a risk. She had to use £15 000 of her redundancy money to get started. If the business failed she would lose most of the £15 000. However, she was well motivated and had experience of decision making and leading a small team in her job at the hospital.

(D)

1 Which **three** of the following qualities are needed by an entrepreneur such as Kim?   **(3 marks)**

> **Guided**

Select **three** answers.

A ☐ Determination

~~B ☐ A Degree in Health and Social Care~~

C ☐ Ability to speak a foreign language

D ☐ Public vehicle driving licence

E ☐ Decision-making skills

F ☐ Planning skills

> It isn't option B because entrepreneurs do not necessarily need an academic qualification to be successful.

(C)

2 If the business is successful, Kim wants to recruit a team of nurses so that the business can expand its customer base. Which **one** of the following qualities would be an additional requirement if Kim were to employ other nurses?   **(1 mark)**

Select **one** answer.

A ☐ Taking risks

B ☐ Independence

C ☐ Determination

D ☐ Leadership

(D)

3 Kim's business made a profit of £46 600 in 2012. She thought she was lucky because: **(1 mark)**

Select **one** answer.

A ☐ there was an ageing population in the UK, suggesting that demand would grow

B ☐ inflation was high

C ☐ a new hospital was opened in a nearby town

D ☐ the variable costs of providing private health care rose

Revenues, costs and profits 1

Philips is a small pottery business which specialises in ceramic plates. It has the following financial information for one month, **January**.

Number of ceramic plates produced and sold	200
Price per pot	£12
Variable cost per pot	£3
Fixed costs per month	£600

1 What are the total costs for Philips during the month?   **(1 mark)**

Select **one** answer.

A ☐ £900

B ☐ £1200

C ☐ £1500

D ☐ £1800

> Students have struggled with exam questions similar to this – **be prepared!** ResultsPlus

> Total costs = total variable costs + fixed costs

2 What is the total revenue for Philips during the month?   **(1 mark)**

Select **one** answer.

A ☐ £1800

B ☐ £2000

C ☐ £2400

D ☐ £2600

3 The following table shows the costs, revenues and profits for Philips for a different two month period. Fill in the **four** blanks (a)–(d) to complete the table.   **(4 marks)**

	June	July
Total revenue	£3000	£3200
Fixed costs	£600	£600
Variable costs	(a) £2200	(c)
Total costs	£2800	(d)
Profit/loss	(b)	£500

> Total costs = fixed + variable costs
>
> Profit = total revenue – total costs

Revenues, costs and profits 2

Philips is a small pottery business which specialises in ceramic plates. It has the following financial information for one month, **January**.

Number of ceramic plates produced and sold	200
Price per pot	£12
Variable cost per pot	£3
Fixed costs per month	£600

1 The owners of Philips decide to try to increase profit.

Which **three** of the actions below will **most likely** achieve this, assuming it sells the same number of plates each month?   **(3 marks)**
Select **three** answers.

> **EXAM ALERT**
>
> Students have struggled with exam questions similar to this – **be prepared!** ResultsPlus

A ☐ Buy cheaper raw materials used to make its products

B ☐ Increase the number of workers employed during the weekend

C ☐ Increase advertising expenditure

D ☐ Increase the sales price of an average pot

E ☐ Buy more expensive raw materials used to make its pots

F ☐ Relocate to cheaper premises

> Eliminate any options that involve increasing expenditure. The question says 'assuming the same number of plates are sold each month' so increasing costs will **not** increase profit.

2 In December Philips makes a loss.

> **Guided**

Which **two** of the following are **most likely** to have caused this?   **(2 marks)**

Select **two** answers.

A ☐ ~~The cost of materials used in production fell~~

B ☐ Sales of plates fell

C ☐ Fixed costs fell

D ☐ Prices were cut, but sales did not rise

E ☐ Advertising attracted customers

> It isn't option A because falls in costs are likely to help the business make a **profit** and prevent a loss.

3 Which of the following is **most likely** to result from Philips making a profit?   **(1 mark)**

Select **one** answer.

A ☐ Cash flow problems might occur

B ☐ Inability to pay wages

C ☐ Default on loan repayment

D ☐ Funds raised for reinvestment

Forecasting cash flows 1

Tees is a small business that prints T-shirts with designs on the front. In January it had the following cash-flow information.

Opening balance	£18 000
Cash inflow	£17 000
Cash outflow	£21 000

C 1 What is the **net cash flow** of the business at the end of January? **(1 mark)**

Select **one** answer.

A ☐ −£4000

B ☐ £1000

C ☐ −£3000

D ☐ £3000

> Net cash flow = inflow − outflow

C 2 What is the **closing balance** for the business at the end of January? **(1 mark)**

Select **one** answer.

A ☐ £17 000

B ☐ £22 000

C ☐ £14 000

D ☐ £15 000

B 3 The business has the following figures in September, October and November.
Fill in the **three** blanks to complete the table. **(3 marks)**

> Guided

	Sept (£)	Oct (£)	Nov (£)
Cash inflow	12 000	(b) 14 000	8000
Cash outflow	19 000	22 000	24 000
Net cash flow	(a)	−8000	−16 000
Opening balance	20 000	13 000	5000
Closing balance	13 000	5000	(c)

> To find the **cash inflow** here subtract **net cash flow** from **cash outflow**.

Forecasting cash flows 2

Tees is a small business that prints T-shirts with designs on the front. Towards the end of the year it started to experience cash flow problems.

C

Guided

1 Which **two** of the following are possible reasons for the **worsening** in cash flow position of the business during this time?   **(2 marks)**

Select **two** answers.

A ☐ ~~Lower spending on stocks of printing ink~~

B ☐ A change in the interest rate on a bank loan from 1% to 2%

C ☐ Reduction in monthly rent on its factory

D ☐ Colder temperatures, leading to reduced demand for T-shirts

E ☐ Favourable trade terms provided by suppliers

> It isn't option A because fewer stocks mean lower costs, which **improve** cash flow.

C

EXAM ALERT

2 Which **two** of the following are the **most likely** ways that Tees could improve its cash flow position in the near future?   **(2 marks)**

Select **two** answers.

A ☐ Agree a discount on materials

B ☐ Increase its spending on advertising

C ☐ Use a mind map to improve financial planning

D ☐ Carry out qualitative market research

E ☐ Make one member of staff redundant

> Students have struggled with exam questions similar to this – **be prepared!** ResultsPlus

> You need to find the **most likely** ways to improve cash flow in the **near future**, so concentrate on **short-term** methods of improving cash flow.

C

3 At a meeting, the owners thought that Tees should try to increase the amount of revenue flowing into the business in an attempt to solve its cash flow problems. It has a good reputation among singers and groups promoting themselves.

Which **two** of the following are the **most likely** ways that Tees could increase its revenue?   **(2 marks)**

Select **two** answers.

A ☐ Pay lower interest rates

B ☐ Offer discount for buying in bulk

C ☐ Take out an advert at local concerts

D ☐ Reduce stock holdings

E ☐ Stop offering a discount at certain times of the year

The business plan

> Deli-Italia Ltd is a small chain of shops in the UK that sells food from Italy. There is an Italian café in each shop. It wants to open two new shops in London. It has prepared a business plan as part of its expansion.

F

1   Which of the following is **most likely** to be included in the business plan?   **(1 mark)**

Select **one** answer.

A   ☐   A copy of the business's headed notepaper

B   ☐   A forecast of cash flow for the two shops

C   ☐   A record of the profits of the two shops

D   ☐   A list of names of customers in the shop

D

2   Which of the following is the **most likely** reason to produce a business plan?   **(1 mark)**

Select **one** answer.

A   ☐   To guarantee shops make a profit

B   ☐   To attract customers to the shops

C   ☐   To reduce the chance of the shops failing

D   ☐   To train new staff in the shops

> A **business plan** is a plan for the development of a business, giving forecasts of items such as sales, profits, costs and cash flow.

B

> Guided

3   Match the information from a business plan with the correct heading from the business plan. Show your answers by drawing a line from the information on the left to the matching heading on the right. If you change your mind about the answer, cross the line out and draw a new line to mark your new answer.   **(4 marks)**

Information		Heading	
Chefs will have experience of cooking Italian dishes	i	A	Production
		B	Overview
A survey found that 65% of people asked said that they would shop or eat at Deli-Italia	ii	C	Sole-trader accounts
		D	Finances
The business will buy its products from two suppliers in Verona and Napoli	iii		
		E	Personnel
The retained profit made by the business last year was £40 000	iv	F	Interest rates
		G	Objectives
The business aims for the shops to be open within two months	v	H	Market research

> This is an example of primary market research.

Obtaining finance 1

Gurrinder is a sole trader who is a designer and decorator. Her business – Be Different – designs offices that will appear different to customers. Her last job was making the inside of a computer design studio look like a computer. She wants to expand into designing shops, factories and even film sets. She knows this will not happen overnight and that she will need long-term sources of finance.

C

Guided

EXAM ALERT

1 As a sole trader, which **three** of the following are **long-term** sources of finance for Gurrinder?
(3 marks)

Select **three** answers.

A ☐ Share capital

B ☐ Grants

C ☐ Trade credit

D ☐ Mortgage

E ☐ Personal savings

F ☐ Overdraft

> Students have struggled with exam questions similar to this – **be prepared!** ResultsPlus

> It isn't option A because share capital is not a source of finance for a **sole trader**.

C

2 Banks providing long-term loans to businesses ask for collateral. Which of the following is **most likely** to be an example of collateral that Gurrinder might use?   **(1 mark)**

Select **one** answer.

A ☐ Any property she owns

B ☐ Cash flow of the business

C ☐ Share capital

D ☐ Trade credit

C

3 Which of the following are **most likely** to be reasons why Gurrinder would use retained profit to finance growth?   **(2 marks)**

Select **two** answers.

A ☐ Collateral would be needed

B ☐ There is no interest to pay back

C ☐ Money can always be raised by issuing new shares

D ☐ It will be a large amount

E ☐ It tends to carry less risk than borrowing

Obtaining finance 2

> Gurrinder is a sole trader who is a designer and decorator. Her business – Be Different – designs offices that will appear unusual and unique to customers. Recently the business has faced cash flow problems.

C

1 What would be the **most appropriate** way that Be Different might cope with its negative cash flow? **(1 mark)**

> **Guided**

Select **one** answer.

A ☐ Sell more shares

B ☐ Arrange an overdraft

C ☐ Use venture capital services

D ☐ Take out a mortgage

> It isn't option D because this is a long-term source of finance.

D

2 Gurrinder has decided to delay payments to suppliers to help her cash-flow position.

What example of short-term finance is this? **(1 mark)**

Select **one** answer.

A ☐ The use of a factor

B ☐ A bank loan

C ☐ Credit card payments

D ☐ Trade credit

D

3 Which of the following is the **most likely** problem that could result from delaying payments to suppliers? **(1 mark)**

Select **one** answer.

A ☐ A reduction in interest payments

B ☐ Greater retained profit

C ☐ Suppliers refusing to give credit

D ☐ Taking on more staff

Customer focus

A clothing shop wanted to find out about the views of its customers. Table 1 shows the results of a question asked to customers.

What is the major factor that attracts you to the shop?

Table 1

	Number of responses
Value for money	28
Has the clothes that I want	36
Friendly staff	20
Well laid out	5
Late opening hours	11

C 1 Identify **two** conclusions that can be drawn from the table about customers' views of the shop. **(2 marks)**

Select **two** answers.

A ☐ The least important factor to customers is the shop's layout

B ☐ Most customers are attracted by value for money

C ☐ Over 30% of customers are attracted by friendly staff

D ☐ Less than 30% of customers are attracted by the type of clothes on sale

E ☐ Opening hours are less important to customers than friendly staff

C 2 The shop wants to improve its customer focus.

Which **two** of the following might be the **most appropriate** methods to help the business anticipate customer needs? **(2 marks)**

> **Guided**

Select **two** answers.

A ☐ Changing the opening hours

B ☐ Only accepting credit cards

C ☐ Retraining staff on using the till

D ☐ A survey about buying habits

E ☐ Visiting a trade fair with the latest designs

> It isn't option B because this is not helping it to predict **in advance** what customers want.

F 3 The shop mainly sells to people aged 14–20. Which of the following is **most likely** to help the shop to meet customer needs? **(1 mark)**

Select **one** answer.

A ☐ Setting prices similar to those of competitors

B ☐ Having no changing rooms to try on clothes

C ☐ Stocking the latest fashions

D ☐ Refusing refunds

> The question asks for the **most likely** option. Although option A might help, some customers might want lower prices and better value for money, so another option is **most likely** to help the shop meet customer needs.

The marketing mix

APPZZ is a small design business that wants to create an app for sports people to be used on the iPad. The app will help sports people measure their activities during exercise.

(F) **1** APPZZ knows that its app must give customers value for money.

Identify the part of the marketing mix to which this relates. **(1 mark)**

Select **one** answer.

A ☐ Price

B ☐ Product

C ☐ Promotion

D ☐ Place

(D) **2** APPZZ hopes to sell the new app on Apple's App Store.

Identify the part of the marketing mix to which this relates. **(1 mark)**

Select **one** answer.

A ☐ Price

B ☐ Product

C ☐ Promotion

D ☐ Place

(C) **3** APPZZ knows that, to be successful, its app must have some unique and attractive functions. It is also concerned about how to make consumers aware about how its app is different to others.

Given this information, which **two** elements of the marketing mix do you think the business should emphasise most? **(2 marks)**

Select **two** answers.

That the app:

A ☐ is the same price as similar apps on the market

B ☐ can be bought and downloaded from Apple's app store

C ☐ can calculate recovery time instantly after exercise

D ☐ will be advertised in national computer magazines

E ☐ will be relatively expensive to develop

Limited liability

Colin Marks worked as a window cleaner in his local area for 15 years. Five years ago he set up QualClean Ltd with two friends. This small business offers cleaning services to offices in towns in the Midlands.

E   **1**   As a sole trader Colin had unlimited liability.   **(1 mark)**

Select **one** answer.

This meant that:

A   ☐   he was liable for the money he put into the business

B   ☐   he had to repay all loans instantly

C   ☐   he took all the profit of the business

D   ☐   he was liable for all debts of the business

E   **2**   Which **three** of the following are the most likely reasons why Colin operated his window-cleaning business as a sole trader?   **(3 marks)**

> **Guided**

Select **three** answers.

A   ☐   ~~He can benefit from limited liability~~

B   ☐   He is likely to face greater risk

C   ☐   He will have greater control of the business

D   ☐   He can take all the profits of the business

E   ☐   He can sells shares to raise money

F   ☐   He would have the ability to make his own decisions

> It isn't option A because sole traders have **unlimited liability**.

D   **3**   Which **two** of the following might be the **most likely** reasons why Colin set up QualClean as a private limited company?   **(2 marks)**

Select **two** answers.

A   ☐   He is only liable for his investment in case of failure

B   ☐   He would be the only owner of the business

C   ☐   Risks can be shared with others

D   ☐   He can raise money on a stock exchange

E   ☐   He can share the profits

Start-up legal and tax issues

Outside Now is a small business that sells specialist outdoor equipment to other businesses. This includes marquees, furniture and stands to activity centres and sports arenas.

C

1   Small businesses might have to pay Corporation Tax. This is a tax on: **(1 mark)**

Select **one** answer.

A ☐ earnings of workers in the business

B ☐ value of sales of the business

C ☐ spending by the business

D ☐ profits made by the business

D

2   Which **two** of the following are taxes that businesses such as Outside Now might have to pay?   **(2 marks)**

> Guided

EXAM ALERT

Select **two** answers.

A ☐ National Insurance Contributions

B ☐ Value Added Tax

C ☐ Distribution Tax

D ☐ Minimum Wage

E ☐ Income Tax

Students have struggled with exam questions similar to this – **be prepared!** ResultsPlus

It isn't option D because this is not a tax.

Some taxes do not have the word 'tax' in their name.

D

3   Which of the following would be the **most likely** reason why Outside Now has to keep a record of its income and spending?   **(1 mark)**

Select **one** answer.

A ☐ To prove that the business is making a profit

B ☐ To prove to HMRC that it is paying the right amount of tax

C ☐ To make sure that any faulty goods can be returned

D ☐ To prove the business has unlimited liability

Customer satisfaction

Jan'll Fix It is a small business run by Janet Dunbar. She repairs a variety of machinery, for businesses and customers, including computers, sewing machines, mobile phones and bread-makers.

F

1 Which of the following is the **most likely** reason why customer service is important to the success of this business? **(1 mark)**

Select **one** answer.

A ☐ Because customers add value

B ☐ Because customers will use the service if the price is right

C ☐ Because it has to meet legal requirements

D ☐ Because it leads to customer loyalty

E

> Guided

2 Janet's business relies on repeat purchases by customers.

Which **two** of the following are most likely to lead to repeat purchases? **(2 marks)**

Select **two** answers.

A ☐ Repairing machines that are less than five years old

B ☐ Charging a premium price

C ☐ Completing repairs when required

D ☐ Offering a discount to regular customers

E ☐ Not accepting deliveries on Saturdays

It isn't option E because this will put off some customers.

E

3 Which **two** of the following are likely to be the **most** effective methods that the business might use to deliver high levels of customer satisfaction? **(2 marks)**

Select **two** answers.

A ☐ Free deliveries to customers after repair

B ☐ Securing repeat purchases by customers

C ☐ Controlling cash flow

D ☐ Setting financial objectives

E ☐ Providing a one-year guarantee on all work

Recruiting, training and motivating

Colin Murphy runs a small travel agency. He has three shops and employs ten people. Colin now wants to hire someone with knowledge of adventure holidays as he thinks this is likely to be a growth area.

D

Guided

EXAM ALERT

1   Which **two** of the following documents are **most likely** to be used in the recruitment process for the new employee?   **(2 marks)**

Select **two** answers.

A   ☐   ~~Cash flow forecast~~

B   ☐   Job description

C   ☐   Business plan

D   ☐   Market map

E   ☐   Application form

Students have struggled with exam questions similar to this – **be prepared!**   ResultsPlus

It isn't option A because a cash flow forecast is not a document used in the **recruitment** process.

D

2   People have been taking fewer holidays over the last two years. Sales have fallen and some staff are becoming demotivated.

Which **two** of the following are **most likely** to motivate staff at the travel agency?   **(2 marks)**

Select **two** answers.

A   ☐   Allowing staff to work flexibly

B   ☐   Opening longer without overtime

C   ☐   Paying piece rates

D   ☐   Paying a bonus if sales increase

E   ☐   Complaining about staff's work

E

3   Colin is preparing a job advertisement for the new position. Which of the following pieces of information in the advertisement would break employment legislation? It states that the person appointed must be: **(1 mark)**

Select **one** answer.

A   ☐   Well organised

B   ☐   Able to work to deadlines

C   ☐   Below 40 years of age

D   ☐   Experienced in the travel industry

Market demand and supply

Cakes 'N' Ice is a small business that makes low-fat cakes for sale at parties, fêtes and festivals. It has recently seen the prices of the ingredients used in its cakes – such as flour, eggs, milk and sugar – increase.

C

1 Demand for ingredients has been high and supply has been low. This is **most likely** to have led to a: **(1 mark)**

Select **one** answer.

A ☐ surplus

B ☐ profit

C ☐ shortage

D ☐ deficit

A

EXAM ALERT

2 Which **three** factors are the **most likely** causes of the rise in price of its ingredients?   **(3 marks)**

Select **three** answers.

> Students have struggled with exam questions similar to this – **be prepared!** ResultsPlus

A ☐ Reports of health benefits of reduced-fat ingredients

B ☐ Lower demand for ingredients

C ☐ Increased profits made by producers of ingredients

D ☐ Bad weather leading to poor harvests for wheat to make flour

E ☐ Greater supply of ingredients by producers

F ☐ Higher demand for ingredients from bakeries

> A rise in price of ingredients can be caused by a fall in supply and / or an increase in demand.

C

3 The business has recently had to cut its prices.

Which **two** of the following are **most likely** to have been a reason for this?   **(2 marks)**

Select **two** answers.

A ☐ Competitors have been raising their prices

B ☐ Lower incomes of people who buy cakes

C ☐ A rise in the price of sugar

D ☐ A fall in the supply of flour

E ☐ Other businesses offering a similar service

The impact of interest rates

Kamran runs a shop that sells mobile phone and computer accessories, such as phone covers, printer paper and back-up disks. He took out a small loan with a variable interest rate when he opened his shop in January 2009.

UNITED KINGDOM INTEREST RATE
Benchmark's Interest Rate

Source: adapted from www.tradingeconomics.com, Bank of England.

A

1   Figure 1 shows UK interest rates over the period 2009–2012.

Which **three** of the following situations are **most likely** to have faced Kamran from the information in the Figure?   **(3 marks)**

Select **three** answers.

A   ☐   Kamran's interest payments would have risen soon after he took out the loan

B   ☐   Interest rates have remained the same for most of the period

C   ☐   Kamran's interest payments would always be the same

D   ☐   The cost of borrowing to Kamran's business is relatively low in 2012

E   ☐   Kamran's interest payments were lower in 2012 than in 2009

F   ☐   Interest rates were 50% lower in January 2012 than in January 2009

A

2   It has been suggested that interest rates might rise in the near future. Which **three** of the following would be the **most likely** effects of this for Kamran's business?   **(3 marks)**

> **Guided**

Select **three** answers.

A   ☐   A fall in sales due to lower levels of consumer spending

B   ☐   New business entering the market to take advantage of the change in interest rates

C   ☐   An increase in costs owing to higher loan repayments

D   ☐   The net cash flow of the business improves

E   ☐   ~~A rise in sales due to higher levels of consumer spending~~

F   ☐   Outflows from net cash flow increase

> It isn't option E because this is likely to occur if interest rates **fall**.

Changes in exchange rates

American Starrz is a small business that imports models of America comic heroes such as Iron Man and Batman. American Starrz buys 200 models a month, which it imports from the USA. Each model costs $30.

1 The exchange rate two years ago was £1 = $2.00.

How much did the business have to pay to buy these models?   **(1 mark)**

Select **one** answer.

A ☐ £6000

B ☐ £3000

C ☐ £4000

D ☐ £1000

> (quantity x price) ÷ exchange rate in $
>
> 200 x $30 = $6000
>
> $6000 ÷ $2 = £

2 This year the exchange rate changed to £1 = $1.50. American Starrz decided to keep the prices charged to UK customers the same.

Identify **two** possible effects of the change in the exchange rate on the business.   **(2 marks)**

Select **two** answers.

A ☐ The costs of buying models from the USA will rise

B ☐ Lower fixed costs for the business

C ☐ Makes it easier for American Starrz to sell models in the UK

D ☐ American Starrz will make lower profits on each sale

E ☐ Increased added value on each model sold by American Starrz

> Students have struggled with exam questions similar to this – **be prepared!**

> A fall in the exchange rate means that £1 will buyer fewer dollars.

3 American Starrz has found a new export market in France for models. The exchange rate is £1 = €1.20.

Which **one** of the following is most likely to be the effect on the business?   **(1 mark)**

Select **one** answer.

A ☐ A £30 model will cost €40 in France

B ☐ A £50 model will cost €60 in France

C ☐ A £60 model will cost €50 in France

D ☐ The cost in euros will be lower than in pounds

The business cycle

> The Water Centre sells spa pools and swimming pools that people have in their back gardens.

B 1 Identify **two** likely effects on The Water Centre of a downturn in the business cycle. **(2 marks)**

Select **two** answers.

A ☐ Less risk of the business becoming insolvent

B ☐ People willing to pay more for pools

C ☐ A smaller pool of unemployed workers to recruit from

D ☐ Lower demand owing to lower incomes

E ☐ Lower prices on pools bought from suppliers

> In a **downturn** consumer confidence and spending is low and businesses are likely to cut costs.

C 2 It has been suggested that there might be a slight upturn in future.

Which of the following would be the **most likely** strategy for the business? **(1 mark)**

Select **one** answer.

A ☐ Cut back on supplies of pools

B ☐ Change the name of the business

C ☐ Take on another sales person

D ☐ Move to smaller premises

B

Guided

3 Match the definition on the left with the correct term on the right. Show your answers by drawing a line from the definition on the left to the matching term on the right. If you change your mind about the answer, cross out the line and draw a new line to mark your new answer. **(5 marks)**

Definition		Term	
A rise in the level of economic activity over a period of time	i	A	Recession
		B	Deficit
A strong increase in the level of economic activity	ii	C	Recovery
		D	Economic growth
When economic activity begins to slow down	iii	E	Downturn
When economic activity begins to rise	iv	F	Surplus
When the level of economic growth is negative (less than the period before) for two successive quarters	v	G	Unemployment
		H	Boom

> This is a definition of **economic growth**.

Business decisions and stakeholders

Justin's café is owned by Justin, his wife and their three relatives. The business employs three staff. In summer, Justin puts out tables and chairs in the pedestrianised street outside the cafe. Justin buys most of his supplies from one local supplier.

D

> Guided

1 Which of the following is **most likely** to be a problem for the business of having stakeholders?

(1 mark)

Select **one** answer.

A ☐ Stakeholders can have different views

B ☐ Stakeholders can have different skills

C ☐ Stakeholders can work for the business

D̶ ̶☐̶ ̶S̶t̶a̶k̶e̶h̶o̶l̶d̶e̶r̶s̶ ̶c̶a̶n̶ ̶p̶u̶t̶ ̶m̶o̶n̶e̶y̶ ̶i̶n̶t̶o̶ ̶t̶h̶e̶ ̶b̶u̶s̶i̶n̶e̶s̶s̶

It isn't option D because this is a **benefit** of having stakeholders.

D

2 Which **three** of the following are **most likely** to be benefits for the business of placing chairs and tables in the street?

(3 marks)

Select **three** answers.

A ☐ The business might want to get suppliers from somewhere else

B ☐ It increases the space available for people to sit in

C ☐ Customers might be attracted as they can smoke outside

D ☐ Rivals could reduce prices to compete against the business

E ☐ People in wheelchairs might find it difficult to get past tables

F ☐ The owners can earn more if sales increase as a result

B

3 Match the stakeholder objective on the left with the type of stakeholder on the right. Show your answers by drawing a line from the stakeholder objective on the left to the stakeholder on the right. If you change your mind about the answer, cross out the line and draw a new line to mark your new answer.

(5 marks)

Objective	
Value for money	i
Good employment conditions	ii
High profits, to get a returns on their shares	iii
Ease of access to a variety of services	iv
Reliable payment for orders	v

	Stakeholder
A	Local community
B	Government
C	Workers
D	Supplier
E	Managers
F	Competitors
G	Customers
H	Owners

Exam skills 1

On this page you can practise answering multiple choice questions.

Abdur Razzak, a sole trader is a joiner. He set up a business in 2007 doing a range of work for domestic customers. However, he got a huge break in 2010 when he fitted a kitchen for a large kitchen retailer in Manchester. As a result of this he now has a contract to fit all the kitchens sold by the retailer in the Greater Manchester area. In 2012, his business made a profit of £98 000. He is now thinking of setting up a franchise operation so that he can expand quickly. He likes the idea of being a franchisor.

B

1   Abdur Razzak operates as a sole trader.

Which **one** of the following taxes must he pay on the profit made by his business?   **(1 mark)**

Select **one** answer.

A   ☐   Value Added Tax

B   ☐   Inheritance Tax

C   ☐   Corporation Tax

D   ☐   Income Tax

C

2   Which **one** of the following terms refers to Abdul if he allows others to trade using his name?

> Guided

Select **one** answer.

A   ☐   Franchisee

B   ☐   Franchisor

C   ☐   Retailer

D   ☐   Sole trader

Use the circled terms in the case study to help you.

F

3   Which **one** of the following is **most likely** to suggest that Abdul is an entrepreneur?   **(1 mark)**

> Guided

Select **one** answer.

A   ☐   He is prepared to work hard

B   ☐   He has a qualification in Business Management

C   ☐   He is prepared to take a risk

D   ☐   He is very wealthy

It isn't option A because there are many examples of hard-working people who are not entrepreneurs.

Exam skills 2

On this page you can practise answering calculation and matching definitions questions.

 B

> **Guided**

1 The following table shows the costs, revenues and profits for a business for the first three months of the year. Fill in the **five blanks** to complete the table.

	January	February	March	
Total receipts	£55 000	(a)	£50 000	**(1 mark)**
Fixed costs	£15 000	(b) £15 000	£15 000	**(1 mark)**
Variable costs	£28 000	£31 000	(c)	**(1 mark)**
Total costs	£43 000	£46 000	(d)	**(1 mark)**
Profit	(e)	£15 000	£13 000	**(1 mark)**

Make sure you understand the data in the table before you work out the blanks. This will help you to tackle the question logically. Here, if you fill in the fixed costs first (b), which are always the same, this will help you to work out the other figures.

 A

2 A business has the following figures about its cash flow for one month

Opening balance	£25 000
Cash inflow	£16 000
Cash outflow	£23 000

> **Guided**

What is the closing balance at the end of the month? Select **one** answer.   **(1 mark)**

A ☐ £18 000

B ☐ £7000

C ☐ –£2000

D ☐ £31 000

£16 000 – £23 000 = –£7000
£25 000 – £7000 =

Work out **net cash flow** first (cash inflow – cash outflow) and then add or take away the figure from the opening balance.

B

3 Match the definition on the left with the correct term on the right. Show your answers by drawing a line from the definition on the left to the matching term on the right. If you change your mind about the answer, cross out the line and draw a new line to mark your new answer.   **(5 marks)**

Definition	
Information expressed as numbers that can be statistically analysed	i
Goods or services bought from businesses abroad	ii
Where owners are not personally responsible for company debts	iii
Finance in exchange for part ownership of the business	iv
A document stating the duties of employees in a business	v

Term	
A	Imports
B	Share capital
C	Qualitative data
D	Job description
E	Limited liability
F	Exports
G	Quantitative data
H	Exchange rate

EXAM ALERT

Students have struggled with exam questions similar to this – **be prepared!** ResultsPlus

Exam skills 3

On this page you can practise answering short course decision questions (in the Unit 6 exam only).

A

EXAM
ALERT

Read the passage below carefully and then answer the following question that relates to the passage.

John runs a landscape-gardening business. He designs interesting gardens with water features, spa baths and coloured paving. John employs five workers, who each have their own skills. John values his workers and does everything he can to ensure he does not have to lay off staff.

Students have struggled with exam questions similar to this – **be prepared!** ResultsPlus

Recently some of the workers have noticed that wages offered in other similar businesses are a little higher than they are paid. They also feel that their skills are not being tested and they have little say in the business.

1   John feels he needs to make a decision about how to improve the motivation of his workers.

   Which of the following methods would you choose if you were John? Justify your choice.

   Option chosen (tick **one** box only)

   ☐   **Choice 1:** Pay them a bonus based on increased sales

   ☐   **Choice 2:** Give them greater responsibility and recognise
      their skills with non-financial rewards   **(6 marks)**

....

....

....

....

....

....

....

....

....

....

There are no right or wrong answers to these questions and you can decide which choice is the most appropriate. You **must** support your decision with appropriate business understanding.

Marketing

Virgin Holidays is a tour operator which flies holidaymakers to destinations such as the USA, the Caribbean, Africa, India and Australia. Marketing is vital to the success of tour operators.

Source: adapted from http://www.virginholidays.co.uk

D

1 (a) Which **one** of the following is the **best** definition of the term '**marketing**'? **(1 mark)**

Select **one** answer.

Marketing is:

A ☐ selling products to customers effectively

B ☑ satisfying customers' needs profitably

C ☐ making a product for the market

D ☐ targeting a certain part of the market

Guided

(b) Explain **one** benefit of effective marketing for Virgin Holidays. **(3 marks)**

> Here is a plan you could use for your answer:
> • Explain what effective marketing means.
> • Explain how effective marketing affects Virgin Holidays, its customers and its sales.

> An 'Explain' question must have three **linked** sentences. Make sure you relate your answer to Virgin Holidays.

Effective marketing is acipaking identify and satiffing customer needs Effective marketing will have increase in sules and more customers would come in Virgin Holidays as it will be targetted to specific customers

E

2 (a) Businesses sometimes divide their markets into different market segments.

State **two** ways in which Virgin Holidays might segment its market. **(2 marks)**

1 ....age..

2 ....time of the holiday taken..

> Remember that explanations are not needed in this type of question.

Guided

(b) Outline **one** method that Virgin Holidays might use to identify the market segments for its holidays. **(3 marks)**

> Here is a plan you could use for your answer:
> • Identify where Virgin Holidays can get information about its customers.
> • Think about what information this will be and what it says about customers.
> • Explain how it is useful to Virgin.

They could carry out a market research to identify where virgin holidays can get information about its customers. Also surveys could help them to know which type of holiday they want

Market research

Tesco is a well-known supermarket. It collects a variety of qualitative and quantitative market research data about its customers.

D

Guided

1 Which **one** of the following is an example of **qualitative** market research data?   **(1 mark)**

Select **one** answer.

A ☐ A chart showing Tesco's sales

B ☐ A map showing all of Tesco's stores in the UK

C ☑ The views of Tesco consumers about late-night opening

D ☐ ~~Tesco sales figures from the last five years.~~

> It isn't option D because this is **quantitative** (numerical) data.

B

Guided

EXAM ALERT

2 Explain how qualitative market research data might allow Tesco to improve its marketing mix.   **(3 marks)**

Here is a plan you could use for your answer:
- Think about what information qualitative data provides about consumers.
- Explain how these views can affect one of the four Ps for Tesco.
- Explain how this will affect Tesco's sales.

> Students have struggled with exam questions similar to this – **be prepared!** ResultsPlus

qualitative data would provide tescos view of customers of the product. This would affect the product as it will help Tescos know what to improve and help Tescos to develope

> Make sure you relate your answer to Tesco.

C

3 Market research helps Tesco to make important decisions about its products and services.

(a) State **two** methods that Tesco might use to collect **primary** market research data.   **(2 marks)**

1 .... Survey ....

2 .... focus group ....

> Remember that explanations are not needed in this type of question.

(b) Identify **one** problem for Tesco when undertaking market research.   **(1 mark)**

.... expensive ....

Guided

(c) Explain **one** problem for Tesco of carrying out market research.   **(3 marks)**

Here is a plan you could use for your answer:
- Explain how the problem affects Tesco's operations.
- Think about how a change in operations could lead to further problems in future.

....

....

....

....

Product trial and repeat purchase

D

1 Product trial is a way in which businesses raise awareness of new products.   **(1 mark)**

Select **one** answer.

> **Guided**

The **most likely** method used to encourage product trial would be:

A ☐ high prices

B̶ ☐ r̶e̶m̶i̶n̶d̶e̶r̶ ̶a̶d̶v̶e̶r̶t̶i̶s̶e̶m̶e̶n̶t̶s̶

C ☐ selling the product online

D ☑ free samples

> It isn't option B because product trial is about buying the product for the first time, not buying it again.

C

2 Businesses that achieve success over a long period encourage customer loyalty and repeat purchases.

(a) What is meant by the term '**repeat purchase**'?   **(2 marks)**

When the customers come to buy the product again when pervisously brough.

(b) Identify **two** methods that a food manufacturer might use to encourage customer loyalty and repeat purchases.   **(2 marks)**

1 Promotions

2 eg: reminder adverts

> **Guided**

(c) Explain **one** reason why a food manufacturer might want to encourage customer loyalty and repeat purchases.   **(3 marks)**

> Here is a plan you could use for your answer:
> * Think about the costs and benefits of repeat purchases against new purchases.
> * Explain how repeat purchases affect sales over time.
> * Explain how continued sales can benefit the business.

> An 'Explain' question must have three **linked** sentences. Make sure you relate your answer to a food manufacturer.

A food manufacturer would want to encourage customer loyalty and repeat purchses because custumer who pervisoulsly borought products would come which will concrue to increase the profit and sales.

Product life cycle 1

The product life cycle in Figure 1 shows sales of a new breakfast cereal over a period of time.

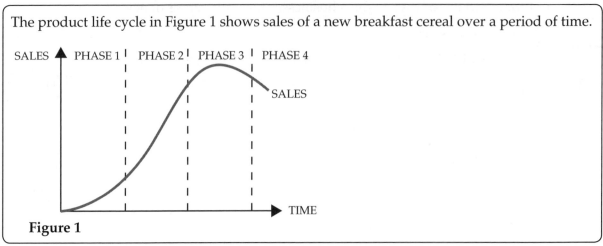

Figure 1

C 1 (a) Look at Figure 1. What is phase 4 called? **(1 mark)**

Select **one** answer.

A ☐ Introduction

B ☐ Growth

C ☐ Maturity

D ☑ Decline

(b) What is meant by the term '**extension strategy**'? **(2 marks)**

extension strategy means that to extend by
adding value to the product so it could the product stages

(c) (i) Identify **two** possible extension strategies that a breakfast cereal manufacturer
might use. **(2 marks)**

1 ...... advertising ......

2 ...... Promotion ......

> Remember that explanations are not needed in this type of question.

(ii) Explain how **one** of the strategies you identified in (i) would
extend the product life cycle of the new breakfast cereal. **(3 marks)**

EXAM ALERT

Guided

Here is a plan you could use for your answer:
- Explain how the strategy would change the product or the operations of the business.
- Explain how this would affect consumers and the market.
- Explain how it would affect sales.

> Students have struggled with exam questions similar to this – **be prepared!** ResultsPlus

> An 'Explain' question must have three **linked** sentences. Make sure you relate your answer to a breakfast cereal.

....

....

....

....

Product life cycle 2

Devlin is a designer and manufacturer of sportswear. It has looked at the growth rates of its products and their relative market share. Figure 1 shows where it has placed four products (men's trainers, women's trainers, men's swimming shorts and women's gym tops) in the Boston Matrix.

Figure 1

C 1 (a) Look at Figure 1. Which of the following describes men's trainers?   **(1 mark)**

Select **one** answer.

A ☐ Star

B ☐ Cash cow

C ☐ Dog

D ☐ Problem child/Question mark

EXAM ALERT

(b) Describe how the use of the Boston Matrix can benefit Devlin.   **(3 marks)**

....

....

....

....

> Students have struggled with exam questions similar to this – **be prepared!** ResultsPlus

B 2 (a) There are over 50 products in Devlin's product portfolio. What is meant by the term **'product portfolio'**?   **(2 marks)**

....

....

Guided (b) Explain one way in which managing its product portfolio can benefit Devlin.   **(3 marks)**

> Here is a plan you could use for your answer:
> • Think about how the life cycles of products can be managed.
> • Think about how different products have different sales.
> • Explain whether products have to be dropped or introduced.

....

....

....

....

Branding and differentiation

In 2012 it was reported that Apple – the maker of iPhones, iMacs and iPads – had overtaken Google as the world's most valuable brand. It was said to be worth £93 billion.

Source: adapted from www.dailymail.co.uk

B

1 (a) What is meant by the term 'brand'? **(2 marks)**

....

....

(b) State **one** advantage and **one** disadvantage to Apple of establishing a strong brand for its products. For each, explain one likely effect on the business. **(8 marks)**

Advantage ....

Explanation ....

....

....

....

....

| There must be at least **two** linked strands of explanation. You must also relate your answer to Apple. |

Disadvantage ....

Explanation ....

....

....

....

....

B

2 (a) Identify **one** way in which Apple could differentiate its products from those of its rivals. **(1 mark)**

....

⟩Guided⟩ **(b)** Explain **one** reason why Apple would want to differentiate its products from those of its rivals. **(3 marks)**

Here is a plan you could use for your answer:
- Think about how customers' views of Apple's products and rival products are affected.
- Explain how these views affect purchases of the business.

....

....

....

| Make sure you relate your answer to Apple. |

Successful marketing mix 1

PlayingZ is a designer and manufacturer of video and online games. It has just launched a product showing sports from the Olympic Games in London 2012. Marketing the new product will be vital to its success.

D

1 (a) The game has a unique playing feature not found on other sports games. What part of the marketing mix is this?   **(1 mark)**

Select **one** answer.

A ☐ Place

B ☐ Price

C ☐ Product

D ☐ Promotion

(b) Identify **three** ways in which PlayingZ could promote its new game.   **(3 marks)**

1 ....

2 ....

3 ....

Guided

(c) Explain **one** reason why promotion is important to the success of the new game for PlayingZ.   **(3 marks)**

> Here is a plan you could use for your answer:
> • Think about why new games need to be promoted.
> • Explain how promotion will affect consumer awareness.
> • Explain how promotion will affect sales.

....

....

....

....

> Make sure you relate your answer to PlayingZ and its video game.

D

2 PlayingZ has decided to charge a similar price to those of rivals for its new game.

Explain **one** benefit for PlayingZ of charging a similar price to those of rivals.   **(3 marks)**

Guided

> Here is a plan you could use for your answer:
> • Explain how consumers will react to similar prices.
> • Explain how PlayingZ and the features of its new game can benefit from this.

....

....

....

....

Successful marketing mix 2

> Next is a clothing retailer. At the end of 2011 it was reported that its online sales had risen by 16.7%, but that sales in its stores had fallen by 2.7% over the period August to December.
>
> Source: adapted from www.bbc.co.uk

D

1 **(i)** Which **one** of the following elements of the marketing mix does selling in stores represent? **(1 mark)**

Select **one** answer.

A ☑ Place

B ☐ Price

C ☐ Product

D ☐ Promotion

> **Guided**

(ii) Explain **one** reason why your answer to (i) is an important aspect of the marketing mix for Next. **(3 marks)**

> Here is a plan you could use for your answer:
> • Think about how customers will be affected.
> • Explain how this could affect sales and profits.

Place is important because place is where customer come and buy the product but if they don't there will be reduce in sales and profit

A

2 Two methods that Next could use to maintain profits when faced with falling sales in stores could be reducing prices or increasing its advertising. Which of these **two** methods do you think would be more effective in allowing Next to maintain its profits and why? **(6 marks)**

> **Guided**

> **EXAM ALERT**

> Here is a plan you could use for your answer:
> • For advertising, think about customer loyalty, market size, added value, competition and cost.
> • For reducing prices, think about customer perceptions, revenue in total and per item, and competition.
> • Consider the effect in the short and long terms on profit.

> Students have struggled with exam questions similar to this – **be prepared!** ResultsPlus

I think advertising will maintain its profit as it will attract new customers and customer loyalty also whereas if they reduce price the the profit will reduce

> For this type of question you must make a judgement about which is the better option. There is no right or wrong answer, but you need to **justify** your choice.

Design and research development

> Dyson is a business that designs and manufactures vacuum cleaners, hand dryers, bladeless fans and heaters. Its design mix is important to the success of its innovative products.
>
> Source: adapted from www.dyson.co.uk

B

1 (i) Identify **one** variable of the design mix. **(1 mark)**

....

> Guided

(ii) Explain how the variable of the design mix identified in (i) can help Dyson to differentiate its products. **(3 marks)**

....

....

....

....

> Make sure you relate your answer to Dyson and have three linked sentences in your answer.

> The Dyson Airblade is a hand dryer, often found in public or restaurant toilets. Its motor produces a stream of air that flows at 400 mph and dries hands more effectively than conventional hand dryers. It was developed in Dyson's Research and Development (R&D) department.

B

2 Explain one benefit of research .... for Dyson. **(3 marks)**

EXAM ALERT

> Here is a plan you ...
> • Think about ...
>   product.
> • Think about how ...
>   to be innovative, s...

> Students have struggled with exam questions similar to this ... **be prepared!** ResultsPlus

> Guided

....

....

....

....

B

3 Businesses such as Dyson often deve.......... ototypes of products as part of the design process.

(a) What is meant by the term '**prototype**'? **(2 marks)**

....

(b) Explain **one** reason why creating a prototype as part of the research and design process can benefit Dyson. **(3 marks)**

....

....

....

Managing stock 1

Cara James and Cole Simmons sell models of vehicles, action figures and animals. The models are bought in separate parts from manufacturers and then assembled and painted before sale. Figure 1 shows a bar gate stock graph for their model of a dinosaur.

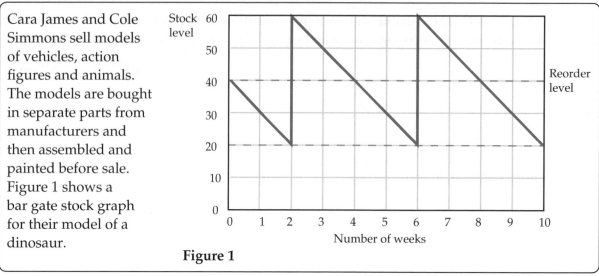

Figure 1

C

1 (a) Which **one** of the following is **least likely** to be stock held by the business?   **(1 mark)**

Select **one** answer.

Stocks of:

A ☐   paint and parts used when assembling the model

B ☐   semi-finished models that need painting

C ☐   damaged models that have been returned

D ☐   finished models ready to be sold

(b) Using the diagram, identify the number of models that Cara and Cole hold as a buffer stock.   **(1 mark)**

....

(c) Use the diagram to calculate how many weeks it will take for stock of dinosaur models to arrive after reordering.   **(2 marks)**

EXAM ALERT

....

....

> Students have struggled with exam questions similar to this – **be prepared!** ResultsPlus

> This can be calculated using the date on which stock is reordered and the date on which it arrives.

Guided

(d) Describe **one** advantage to Cara and Cole of holding large stocks of models.   **(3 marks)**

....

....

....

....

....

> Here is a plan you could use for your answer:
> • Think about why large stocks might be needed or how buying large stocks can save money.
> • Describe how the business benefits from holding large stocks.

Managing stock 2

Mintchell's manufactures cycles that it sells to cycle retailers. It makes fold-away cycles for shopping as well as BMX bikes and racing cycles used in competitions. The business has reviewed its stock ordering system and has decided to use a just-in-time (JIT) method of stock control.

C　1　(a)　What is meant by the term 'just-in-time stock control'?　　　**(2 marks)**

....

....

....

Guided

EXAM ALERT

(b)　State **one** advantage and **one** disadvantage to Mintchell's of adopting a just-in-time (JIT) method of stock control. For each, explain one likely effect on Mintchell's.　**(8 marks)**

Here is a plan you could use for your answer:	Students have struggled with exam questions similar to this
• Explain how it will affect costs, profits, stocks and storage.	**– be prepared!** ResultsPlus

Advantage ....

Explanation ....

....

....

....

....

....

> There must be at least **two** linked strands of explanation and you must relate your answer to Mintchell's.

Here is a plan you could use for your answer:
• Explain how it will affect risk, demand, ability to change and the brand name.

Disadvantage ....

Explanation ....

....

....

....

....

Managing quality

Panasonic is an electronics business that makes products such as televisions, camcorders and cameras, blue-ray players, PCs and home appliances. In 2012 it launched the Panasonic GT50 plasma TV with improved quality and design features.

Source: adapted from www.panasonic.co.uk

D

1 (a) What is meant by the term 'quality'?   **(2 marks)**

....

....

(b) Explain **one** benefit for Panasonic of having quality products.   **(3 marks)**

....

....

....

> Make sure you relate your answer to Panasonic.

A

2 Having a quality-control system or a culture of quality assurance are two methods that a business manufacturing electronics products could try in order to improve quality.

> Guided

(a) Which of the following is **most likely** to be associated with quality control in an electronics company such as Panasonic?   **(1 mark)**

Select **one** answer.

A ☐   The target is zero defects

B ☐   A Kaizen system of continuous improvement is used

C ☐   All employees are responsible for quality

D ☐   Products are checked after manufacture

> It isn't option C because this relates to **quality assurance**.

(b) Which of the **two** methods – a quality-control system or a culture of quality assurance – do you think would be more successful and why?   **(6 marks)**

> Guided

Here is a plan you could use for your answer:
• For quality control think about the cost and the problems of checking at the end.
• For a culture of quality assurance think about costs, effect on staff and regulation.
• Consider the type of business and whether the benefits outweigh the costs over time.

....

....

....

....

....

....

> There is no right or wrong answer and you must make a judgement about which is the better option. Make sure you **justify** your answer.

Cost-effective operations and competitiveness

Compartmentals is a manufacturer of furniture. It has recently found its costs rising and part of its market being taken by new businesses.

A* 1 **(a)** Identify **one** method Compartmentals can use to reduce costs.   **(1 mark)**

....

> Remember that explanations are not needed in this type of question.

Guided **(b)** Explain **one** way in which reducing costs will help Compartmentals to become more competitive.

> Here is a plan you could use for your answer:
> • Explain how Compartmentals could change its operations as a result of lower costs and how this would affect the business.

....

....

....

....

....

> An 'Explain' question must have three **linked** sentences. Make sure you relate your answer to Compartmentals.

Guided **(c)** Setting competitive prices or improving productivity are two ways in which a business such as Compartmentals might compete against rivals.

Which of these **two** methods do you think would be more effective in improving the competitiveness of Compartmentals and why?   **(6 marks)**

> Here is a plan you could use for your answer:
> • Think about how the options might affect consumers, rivals, output, costs and profits.
> • Consider how rivals might react.
> • Make a judgement about which option will make Compartmentals more competitive immediately and over time.

Method ....

Reason ....

....

....

....

....

....

....

> For this type of question you must make a judgement about which is the better option. There is no right or wrong answer but you must **justify** your decision.

51

Effective customer service

RightOnTime Cabs is a taxi business in the north-west. It prides itself on never being more than two minutes late to pick up any passengers. There are eight other taxi firms within a five-mile radius of its location and it recognises the need for effective customer service.

D

1 (a) Which of the following is **most likely** to lead to an improved service?   **(1 mark)**

Select **one** answer.

A ☐ Promising never to be more than 10 minutes late

B ☑ Giving passengers an arrival time and sticking to it

C ☐ Limiting the distance it is willing to take passengers

D ☐ Changing an advertisement on the outside of the taxi

(b) Other than any in (a), identify **two** ways in which RightOnTime Cabs could improve its service to customers.   **(2 marks)**

1 ..... Spotting problems and dealing wit it .....

2 ..... To innovate gradually .....

A

2 The owners have considered a number of ways to improve their customer service. They hope that an improved service will gain them a competitive advantage.

* Assess how improved customer service could help RightOnTime Cabs to achieve this.

(8 marks)

....

....

....	In this question you must make a judgement about the extent to which offering an improved service can allow RightOnTime Cabs to gain a competitive advantage and **justify** your decision. You must consider the advantages and/ or disadvantages of offering an improved service.

Consumer protection laws

Mixon is a company that produces a range of products for people aiming to lose weight. These include sugar substitutes, main meals, snacks, drinks and desserts. Its latest product is a quiche. The advertising for this new product uses the phrases:

- 'made only from natural ingredients'
- 'ideal for vegetarians'
- 'perfect as part of a diet for those looking to lose weight'
- 'ideal for a quick lunch'

It has been suggested that the fat content of the quiche is only slightly lower than those of supermarket brands. Also, in one variety, it uses a meat substitute.

C 1 Identify **one** consumer protection law that Mixon will have to adhere to.   **(1 mark)**

....

A* 2 * Using your knowledge of consumer protection laws, is Mixon right to use these phrases in the advertising of its new product? Justify your answer.   **(10 marks)**

In this question you must make a judgement about whether it is right or not for Mixon to use these phrases and **justify** your decision. You must consider the advantages and/or disadvantages to Mixon and its customers.

....

....

....

....

....

....

....

....

....

....

....

....

....

....

....

....

Improving cash flow

> Jayston Printing is a company that prints posters, magazines and leaflets. It has recently bought some new machinery with a loan, but has had problems owing to late payment by customers.

C

1 (a) Which of the following is a cash outflow from Jayston Printing?   **(1 mark)**

Select **one** answer.

A ☐   Encouraging customer payment

B ☐   Sales revenue

C ☐   Receiving a bank loan

D ☐   Purchasing assets

(b) Explain **one** reason why a strong cash flow is important to a business such as Jayston Printing.   **(3 marks)**

....

....

....

....

> Make sure you relate your answer to Jayston Printing.

B

Guided

2 Delaying payments to suppliers is one method of improving cash flow. State **one** advantage and **one** disadvantage to Jayston Printing of delaying payments to suppliers. For each, explain **one** likely effect on Jayston Printing.   **(8 marks)**

> Here is a plan you could use for your answer:
> • Explain how it will affect spending and the time of payment.

Advantage ....

Explanation ....

....

....

....

> There must be at least **two** strands of explanation and you must relate your answer to Jayston Printing.

> Here is a plan you could use for your answer:
> • Explain how it will affect reputation, relationships and the costs at payment.

Disadvantage ....

Explanation ....

....

....

....

Improving profit

Primark is a clothing retailer and one of the most successful stores in recent years. In 2012 it announced its first fall in profits for 10 years. One factor was the cost of cotton used in its products.

Source: adapted from www.telegraph.co.uk

D

1 (a) Which of the following is **most likely** to lead to an increase in profits in the short term? **(1 mark)**

   A ☐ Stable energy prices

   B ☐ Higher sales of products

   C ☐ A rise in material costs

   D ☐ More workers being employed

   (b) What is meant by the term 'profit'? **(2 marks)**

   ....

   ....

C

2 One method that Primark could use to increase its profit could be to reduce its labour costs. Explain **one** disadvantage to Primark of cutting labour costs. **(3 marks)**

> **Guided**

Here is a plan you could use for your answer:
• Explain the effect on staff feelings, efficiency of stores and views of customers.

An 'Explain' question must have three **linked** sentences. Make sure you relate your answer to Primark.

   ....

   ....

   ....

   ....

C

3 Increasing revenue is another method that Primark could use to increase profits. Outline **one** method Primark might use to increase revenue and so increase its profits. **(3 marks)**

> **Guided**

EXAM ALERT

Here is a plan you could use for your answer:
• Identify the method.
• Outline how the method can affect the business and its customers, perhaps using an example.

Students have struggled with exam questions similar to this – **be prepared!** ResultsPlus

   ....

   ....

   ....

   ....

Break-even charts

Yffects is a small recording studio that offers bands and singers a chance to record a CD. It has constructed the break-even chart shown in Figure 1. It charges customers £500 for a session to record their CD.

- Its fixed costs are £4000.
- Variable costs are £250 a session.

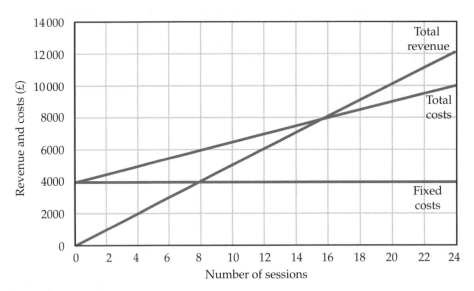

Figure 1 Break-even per month

C 1 **(a)** The business breaks even at a level of output where: **(1 mark)**

Select **one** answer.

A ☐ total profit = total costs

B ☐ total fixed costs = total revenue

C ☐ total variable costs = total fixed costs

D ☐ total revenue = total costs

(b) Using Figure 1, identify the number of sessions that the business needs to sell in order to break even. **(1 mark)**

....

(c) What would be the total revenue of the business if it sold 20 sessions a month? **(1 mark)**

....

(d) Use the diagram to calculate the profit if the business sold 24 sessions a month. **(2 marks)**

....

....

....

Break-even analysis

> Yffects is a small recording studio that offers bands and singers a chance to record a CD. It charges customers £500 for a session to record their CD.
>
> - Its fixed costs are £4000.
> - Variable costs are £250 a session.

A 1 (a) Yffects thinks its price is too low compared with other studios. It has decided to increase its price to £570 per session. Calculate the break-even point. **(4 marks)**

....

....

....

....

(b) Explain **one** way in which Yffects might use break-even analysis. **(3 marks)**

....

....

....

....

....

> An 'Explain' question must have three **linked** sentences. Make sure you relate your answer to Yffects.

A 2 Yffects wants to consider how its margin of safety is affected by changes in the business.

(a) Which of the following is **most likely** to increase the margin of safety? **(1 mark)**

Select **one** answer.

A ☐   A fall in fixed costs

B ☐   A fall in price

C ☐   A fall in sales

D ☐   A rise in variable costs

Guided (b) Explain the relevance of the margin of safety to Yffects. **(3 marks)**

> Here is a plan you could use for your answer:
> - Explain how the margin of safety is related to changes in demand, prices and costs.
> - Explain how the margin of safety can be used in planning, expanding the business or borrowing.

....

....

....

....

Financing growth

Pret A Manger is a sandwich chain. In 2012 it revealed plans to open 24 more sites in the UK in 2012 and 20 overseas. Its profits were up 14% to £52.4m in the previous year.

Source: adapted from www.pret.com

C

1 **(a)** Which of the following is an **internal** source of finance?   **(1 mark)**

Select **one** answer.

> **Guided**

A ☐ ~~A loan from the bank~~

B ☐ A stock-market flotation

C ☐ Selling assets

D ☐ Venture capital

> It isn't option A because this is from **outside** the business.

(b) Give **one** advantage of using retained profit as a way of financing growth for a business such as Pret A Manger.   **(1 mark)**

....

> **Guided**

(c) Explain **one** likely effect on Pret A Manger of using retained profit as a means of financing growth.   **(3 marks)**

Here is a plan you could use for your answer:
• Explain how retained profit can benefit the business.
• Explain how this can help the plans for the business.

....

....

....

....

....

> Make sure you relate your answer to Pret a Manger.

D

2 Explain **one** disadvantage to a business such as Pret A Manger of borrowing money from a bank to finance expansion.   **(3 marks)**

> **Guided**

> **EXAM ALERT**

Here is a plan you could use for your answer:
• Identify one problem to the business of borrowing.
• Explain how this can affect costs, risk or the chances of success.

> Students have struggled with exam questions similar to this – **be prepared!** ResultsPlus

....

....

....

....

....

Organisational structure

Chisel Newton is a food manufacturer with five sites in different UK locations. Work is often delegated at the business. Recently it has experienced problems in managing the five sites. It is looking at the span of control in its hierarchy.

C 1 **(a)** Which of the following is the **best** description of the 'span of control' in a business?

(1 mark)

Select **one** answer.

A ☐   The different levels of the hierarchy

B ☐   The number of people who report to a superior

C ☐   The right for workers to take responsibility

D ☐   The path through which orders are passed down

(b) What is meant by the term '**hierarchy**' in a business?   **(2 marks)**

....

....

(c) Identify **two** reasons why Chisel Newton might delegate work.   **(2 marks)**

1 ....

2 ....

> Remember that explanations are not needed in this type of question.

A 2 Chisel Newton has always had a decentralised decision-making structure in its five sites. As a result of the problems, head office has decided to change its organisational structure so that decisions are now more centralised.

Guided

State **one** advantage and **one** disadvantage to Chisel Newton of centralised decision making. For each, explain **one** likely effect on Chisel Newton.   **(8 marks)**

> Here is a plan you could use for your answer:
> • Explain how it will affect decisions and control.
> • Explain how it will affect workers and the business.

Advantage ....

Explanation ....

....

....

....

> There must be at least **two** linked strands of explanation and you must also relate your answer to Chisel Newton.

Disadvantage...

Explanation ....

....

....

....

Motivation theory

Carltens is a small chain of cafes in the Midlands. Faced with competition from coffee shops such as Starbucks, Costa and Caffè Nero, it has decided to look at ways to improve staff motivation.

D 1 (a) What is meant by the term 'motivation'? **(2 marks)**

....

....

(b) Which of the following is **most likely** to lead to an increase in worker motivation? **(1 mark)**

Select **one** answer.

A ☐ An increased workload without a rise in pay

B ☐ Being passed over for promotion

C ☐ Being praised for work supervising a key operation

D ☐ Working with a coffee machine that needs constant repair

(c) Identify **two** factors other than in (b) that could improve the motivation of workers in a business. **(2 marks)**

....

....

B 2 Discuss **two** benefits to Carltens of improved motivation of its employees. **(6 marks)**

....

....

....

....

....

....

....

....

....

....

....

> In this question you must make a judgement about the extent to which improved staff motivation will benefit Carltens and which benefit is most important and **justify** your decision. Consider the benefits and drawbacks to Carlten and its stakeholders. Your answer must be in context.

Communication

The Colquit family started its first bakery over 40 years ago. It has recently expanded and now has over 30 stores in villages and small towns in the south-west. The CrustCake Bakery is keen to ensure that the same high standard is maintained in all its shops. With expansion and the need for more workers the business experienced communication problems. Sometimes changes to ingredients were not sent to all shops and quality fell. At other times there was too much information, instructions were ignored and deliveries were late. Customers started to shop at other places.

C

1 (i) Identify **two** barriers to communication in The CrustCake Bakery.   **(2 marks)**

1 ....

2 ....

(ii) Explain how **one** of the barriers identified in **(i)** can affect the communication process.
                                                                                                                          (3 marks)

....

....

....

A*

2 *Using your knowledge of business, assess the importance of good communication to a
company such as The CrustCake Bakery.   **(10 marks)**

> **Guided**

EXAM ALERT

Here is a plan you could use for your answer:
* Consider the advantages of good communication to The CrustCake Bakery.
* Consider whether the goal of good communication is more important than other goals, such as maintaining the brand name, improving cash flow or lowering prices.
* Explain which benefit of clear communication will be most significant for The CrustCake Bakery.
* Make a judgement as to the importance of clear channels of communication to a business such as The CrustCake Bakery.

Students have struggled with exam questions similar to this – **be prepared!** ResultsPlus

....

....

....

....

....

....

....

....

....

In this question you must make a judgement about the importance of clear channels of communication and which benefit or cost is most important to the business. Make sure you relate your answer to The CrustCake Bakery and **justify** your decision.

Remuneration

> Results Now! is an online tutoring service. It offers help to students who need extra guidance for specific examinations in a range of subjects. It has five permanent staff at its office. Two deal with customer enquiries and sales. The other three handle the website and online issues. They are all paid a salary and receive a bonus related to profit. Its specialists, who offer tutoring advice, are freelance, and are paid by the hour.

C

1 (a) Which of the following **best** describes the term 'salary'?   **(1 mark)**

Select **one** answer.

A ☐   An annual payment paid in equal instalments

B ☐   An extra payment for work

C ☐   A reward based on success

D ☐   A payment for every hour worked

EXAM ALERT

(b) Identify **two** other methods of remuneration, apart from salaries, bonuses and payment by the hour, that a business could use to reward employees.   **(2 marks)**

1 ....

2 ....

> Students have struggled with exam questions similar to this – **be prepared!** ResultsPlus

> Remember that remuneration is a **payments system**.

Guided

(c) Explain **one** advantage to Results Now! of paying its staff using a bonus scheme.   **(3 marks)**

> Here is a plan you could use for your answer:
> • Explain how staff will react.
> • Explain how the business will be affected.

....

....

....

....

> An 'Explain' question must have three **linked** sentences. Make sure you relate your answer to Results Now!

(d) Explain **one** disadvantage to Results Now! of paying workers by the hour.   **(3 marks)**

....

....

....

....

Ethics in business

> Cafédirect is the UK's largest 100% Fairtrade drinks brand. It guarantees to pay above the world market price for coffee and it supports the development of producers. Since 2006, it has invested more than £4 million of its profits directly into the businesses and paid more than £12.9 million towards the businesses and communities of its grower partners. In 2012 it set two targets for packaging:
>
> - 100% of packaging to be easily recyclable or compostable by the end of 2012
> - the overall amount of material used to package products (measured by weight) to be reduced by an average of 15% by 2015.
>
> Source: adapted from www.cafedirect.co.uk and en.wikipedia.org/wiki/Cafedirect

D 1 Identify **two** disadvantages to a business such as Cafédirect of acting ethically.   **(2 marks)**

1 ....

2 ....

> Remember that explanations are not needed in this type of question.

C 2 (i) Identify **one** advantage to Cafédirect of being an ethical business.   **(1 mark)**

....

(ii) Explain how the advantage identified in (i) might affect Cafédirect.   **(3 marks)**

....

....

....

> The Real Bread Campaign is a UK pressure group that campaigns for producers to declare exactly what goes into bread production, challenges misleading marketing and helps to raise awareness about additives. It campaigns and lobbies for bread that gives nourishment, flavour, digestibility and sustainability.   Source: adapted from www.sustainweb.org

C 3 (a) Identify **two** methods that a pressure group such as The Real Bread Campaign could use to influence producers of bread.   **(2 marks)**

1 ....

2 ....

Guided (b) Explain **one** way in which a bread manufacturer might be affected by a successful pressure-group campaign.   **(3 marks)**

EXAM ALERT

> Here is a plan you could use for your answer:
> - Explain how customers might react and how this could affect the business.

> Students have struggled with exam questions similar to this – **be prepared!** ResultsPlus

....

....

....

> Make sure you **explain** how a bread manufacturer is affected by a pressure group. It is not enough to give just an example of a successful pressure group.

....

Environmental issues

> In 2010 United Kingdom Office Solutions (UKOS) was voted top of the *Sunday Times* Green List, which contains companies improving their environmental performance. UKOS provides office stationery and supplies for business, such as pads, files, binders, paper, storage, equipment and print services.
>
> Source: adapted from http://bestgreencompanies.thesundaytimes.co.uk

C 1 (i) Identify **three** methods that a business such as UKOS might use to reduce its effect on the environment. **(3 marks)**

1 ....

2 ....

3 ....

(ii) Explain how **one** of the methods identified in (i) can reduce the impact UKOS has on the environment. **(3 marks)**

....

....

....

> Choose one of the points you identified in the first part of the question. Make sure you relate your answer to UKOS.

A 2 * Assess **two** possible benefits to UKOS of reducing the effects of its operations on the environment. **(8 marks)**

....

....

....

....

....

....

> In this question you must make a judgement about the importance of minimising environmental effects, and which benefit is most important and **justify** your decision. Consider the advantages or disadvantages to UKOS and its stakeholders.

....

....

....

....

....

....

....

....

....

Economic issues affecting international trade

In 2011 UK businesses exported £7 billion of products to China, a 20% increase on the previous year. They also exported £4.6 billion to India. This was an increase of 45% from the previous year.

Source: adapted from www.guardian.co.uk

C

1 (a) Which of the following is **most likely** to be an export from the UK to India? **(1 mark)**

Select **one** answer.

> Guided

A ☐ Indian products sold in the UK

B ☐ An Indian factory buying UK made machinery

C ☐ Ford cars brought into the UK

D ☐ ~~Buying ingredients from a business in India.~~

It isn't option D because money goes **out** of the UK.

(b) A tariff can affect products that are bought and sold abroad.

What is meant by the term '**tariff**'? **(2 marks)**

....

....

B

(c) (i) Other than a tariff, identify **two** economic factors that could influence the volume of UK exports to countries such as China and India. **(2 marks)**

1 ....

2 ....

> Guided

(ii) Explain how **one** of the factors identified in (i) can affect a UK export business.

(3 marks)

Here is a plan you could use for your answer:
• Think about the restrictions or how changes in an economy can affect trade.
• Explain the effects of these on sales of a UK business in that country.

An 'Explain' question must have three **linked** sentences. Make sure you relate your answer to a UK export business.

....

....

....

....

Government and the EU

From 1st October 2012 the UK National Minimum Wage increased by 2.5%, to £6.19 an hour, in response to recommendations by the Low Pay Commission. It indicated that the low rise was to help businesses faced with difficult economic conditions. The Trade Union Congress (TUC) welcomed the rise, saying it would help at least 900 000 employees. A spokesperson from Unison, the public sector union, said that while the rise provided a welcome cushion for some people, the level of inflation (4%) meant that many would still remain in poverty.

Source: adapted from www.direct.gov.uk, www.tuc.org.uk

C

1 (i) Identify **two** government taxes that might affect UK businesses.   **(2 marks)**

1 ....

2 ....

   (ii) Explain how **one** of the taxes identified in (i) could affect UK consumers.   **(3 marks)**

....

....

....

A*

EXAM ALERT

2 * Using your knowledge of business, assess whether it is right for the government to increase the National Minimum Wage.   **(10 marks)**

....

....

....

....

....

....

....

....

....

....

....

....

....

....

....

Students have struggled with exam questions similar to this – **be prepared!** ResultsPlus

In this question you must make a judgement about whether it is right or not for the government to increase the National Minimum Wage and **justify** your decision. You must consider the advantages or disadvantages to the business and workers. Your answer must be in context.

Exam skills 1

On this page you can practise answering 1 to 3 mark questions.

E

1 Business finance can come from internal and external sources. Which of the following is an external source of finance?   **(1 mark)**

> **Guided**

Select **one** answer.

A ☐ ~~Owners' funds~~

B ☐ Selling assets

C ☐ Retained profit

D ☐ An overdraft

> It isn't option A because this is money that comes from someone **within** the business.

C

2 Identify **two** problems of excessive communications for a business.   **(2 marks)**

1 ....

2 ....

> Remember that explanations are not needed in this type of question.

D

3 What is meant by the term '**reorder level**'?   **(2 marks)**

....

....

B

4 Describe why product differentiation is important to the success of a business such as Ford.
                                                                                   (3 marks)

EXAM ALERT

....

....

....

....

> Students have struggled with exam questions similar to this – **be prepared!** ResultsPlus

B

5 Sony is a manufacturer of electronic equipment.

Explain **one** benefit of research and development to a company such as Sony.   **(3 marks)**

> **Guided**

> Here is a plan you could use for your answer:
> • Explain how it can affect the products of the business, its costs and its prices.
> • Consider the effects of these on the business itself, customers and rivals.

....

....

....

....

Exam skills 2

On this page you can practise answering 6 mark questions.

Melanie owns a flower shop. She imports flowers from Holland fresh every day. The economy has experienced a downturn in recent years and the number of customers has fallen. Melanie is considering reducing sales prices or cutting costs as a means of improving profit.

A

1   Which of these two methods do you think would be most effective in improving the profit of Melanie's business and why?   **(6 marks)**

Method ....

Reason ....

....

....

....

....

....

....

....

> For this type of question you must make a judgement about which method is most important and **justify** your decision. You could consider the advantages and disadvantages of one method or compare the two methods.

A*

2   Discuss the importance of non-financial rewards as a method of motivating workers.

(6 marks)

EXAM ALERT

....

....

> Students have struggled with exam questions similar to this – **be prepared!** ResultsPlus

....

....

....

....

....

....

....

> For this type of question you must make a judgment about the **extent** to which non-financial methods can motivate workers.

Exam skills 3

On this page you can practise answering 8 and 10 mark questions.

The Co-operative group was named among the world's most ethical companies in 2012.

A*

EXAM ALERT

1 * Assess **two** possible benefits to the business of being an ethical company.   **(8 marks)**

....

....

....

....

....

....

....

....

....

....

....

Students have struggled with exam questions similar to this – **be prepared!** ResultsPlus

For this type of question you must make a judgement about which of the two benefits is more important and **justify** your decision. Make sure your answer relates to the Co-operative group.

A*

2 * Using your knowledge of business, to what extent can a company satisfy the needs of all of its stakeholders? Justify your answer.   **(10 marks)**

....

....

....

....

....

....

For this type of question you must make a judgement about whether it is right or not that a business can satisfy all the needs of its stakeholders and **justify** your decision.

....

....

....

....

....

....

Trade-offs

Welham Park Council is under pressure to improve local services. Three projects have been shortlisted, each of which would cost £5 million. The three projects, listed in order of preference, are:

1 Renovate a derelict block of flats to provide 100 new council homes.

2 Convert a disused warehouse into a new, multi-purpose community centre.

3 Repair potholes and upgrade roads after the harsh winter of 2011.

C

1 (a) Which of the following best defines the term 'opportunity cost'? **(1 mark)**

Select **one** answer.

A ☐ The amount of money paid for a scarce resource

B ☐ The average cost of supplying a product

C ☐ The value of the next-best alternative sacrificed

D ☐ The choice faced by a decision maker when choosing between different alternatives

EXAM ALERT

(b) Describe **two** trade-offs Welham Park Council faces when deciding which project to fund. **(4 marks)**

....

....

....

....

....

....

....

Students have struggled with exam questions similar to this – **be prepared!** ResultsPlus

Make sure that you identify **two** trade-offs and describe them both.

Guided

(c) Explain the opportunity cost to Welham Park Council of providing 100 new homes. **(3 marks)**

Here is a plan you could use for your answer:
• Identify the next-best alternative.
• Explain what will be lost by choosing to provide 100 homes.

....

....

....

....

An 'Explain' question must have three **linked** sentences. Make sure you relate your answer to Welham Park Council.

Raising and lowering prices

In the north-west town of Southport there are 100 restaurants. Competition is fierce as each restaurant tries hard to attract customers from local residents, business people, day-trippers and other visitors.

B

1 (a) The demand for restaurant services in Southport is price-sensitive. If a particular restaurant lowers its prices, what is the likely outcome?   **(1 mark)**

Select **one** answer.

A ☐ Total revenue will rise

B ☐ Demand will fall

C ☐ Average costs will fall

D ☐ Productivity will rise

Guided

(b) Explain **one** reason why demand for restaurant services in Southport is price-sensitive.

(3 marks)

> Here is a plan you could use for your answer:
> • Consider the level of competition in the market.
> • Explain what will happen if one restaurant tries to raise prices.

....

....

....

....

(c) Restaurants, like all other businesses and residents in Southport, are supplied by North West Water. There is no other supplier of water in the area.

Explain why the demand for water in the north-west is price-insensitive.   **(3 marks)**

....

....

....

....

> Consider whether North West Water is a monopolist.

Stakeholders

BHP Billiton is an Anglo-Australian multinational mining, oil and gas company. It is the world's largest mining company and made a profit of US$21.7 billion in 2011. In 2012, workers at some mines in Queensland, Australia went on strike in protest over their working conditions. They wanted an extra break for night-shift workers, and more family-friendly shifts. According to a management spokesman, the strikes were expected to affect supplies to customers.

D

1 (a) One important stakeholder group in BHP Billiton is shareholders. What is likely to be the key interest of shareholders in BHP Billiton?   **(1 mark)**

Select **one** answer.

A ☐   The profit made by the business

B ☐   Staff turnover

C ☐   Employees' working conditions

D ☐   The generation of employment in new mines

EXAM ALERT

(b) Identify **two** other stakeholders (in addition to shareholders) in BHP Billiton.   **(2 marks)**

1 ....

2 ....

> Students have struggled with exam questions similar to this – **be prepared!** ResultsPlus

(c) (i) State **two** conflicts that might exist between two stakeholder groups in this case study.   **(2 marks)**

1 ....

2 ....

C

(ii) Describe how shareholders might be affected by **one** of the conflicts you stated in **(i)**.
                                                                                             (4 marks)

> **Guided**

Here is a plan you could use for your answer:
• Consider the key interest that shareholders have in BHP Billiton.
• Describe how this interest might be affected by strike action.
• You could also consider the possible longer-term effects on sales.

....

....

....

....

....

....

....

Hidden costs or benefits

In 2012, Tesco submitted planning permission for a 682-square-metre Metro supermarket on the former Esso service station site in Ashtead, Surrey. The development also involved the construction of nine flats above and nine parking spaces for these flats. A local protest group raised objections. They said the store was too large for the site, mainly because there would be too much traffic and inadequate parking space. They also said the store would not meet the council's targets for sustainability (e.g. construction and renewable energy standards).

The development of the new Tesco is likely to have negative externalities.

C

1 (a) Which **one** of the following best defines a '**negative externality**'?   **(1 mark)**

Select **one** answer.

> Guided

A ☐   A financial cost to a firm when investing in a new business venture

B ☐   ~~The benefits to a third party of a business venture~~

> It isn't option B because this defines a positive externality.

C ☐   The cost to the government of business activity

D ☐   A cost arising from business activity paid by those outside the firm

(b) Give **one** example of a possible positive externality in this case.   **(1 mark)**

....

A

2 Discuss whether you think that planning permission should be given for the development of the Metro supermarket in Ashtead.   **(6 marks)**

> Guided

Here is a plan you could use for your answer:
• Explain that business activity can affect third parties.
• Identify and explain one or two possible negative externalities.
• Identify and explain one or two possible positive externalities.
• Make a judgement – remember there is no wrong or right answer.

....

....

....

....

....

....

....

> For this type of question you must make a judgement about whether planning permission should be given for the development. Make sure you **justify** your decision.

73

Measuring success

Marks & Spencer (M&S) is a large retailer specialising in the sale of clothing and food products. In 2011 its profit rose to £598.6 million – up from £523 million in 2010. The company claims to be socially responsible. For example, during 2011, M&S donated money, food, equipment and clothes to charities, reduced some energy costs by 25%, and adopted a plan to stop sending waste to landfill sites. Businesses such as M&S try to develop competitive advantages over rivals.

C

Guided

1 (a) Which **one** of the following is an important feature of competitive advantages? **(1 mark)**

Select **one** answer.

A ☐ They must be focused on cutting costs

B ☐ They need to be defensible and distinctive

C ☐ They are designed to make a business more socially responsible

D ☐ ~~They must involve raising productivity~~

> It isn't option D because competitive advantages do not **have** to result from rising productivity.

(b) State **two** ways of measuring success in a business.　　　　**(2 marks)**

1 ....

2 ....

(c) Explain **one** reason why M&S might be considered successful.　　**(3 marks)**

....

....

....

....

> You could consider the financial success or the social success of M&S. You need three **linked** sentences in your answer.

C

Guided

2 Explain **one** way in which a business can improve its social success.　**(3 marks)**

Here is a plan you could use for your answer:
• Explain social success.
• Use some examples of social responsibility.

....

....

....

....

Causes of business failure

GHP Contractors Ltd was a small construction company. In 2012, the company stopped trading because it ran out of cash. The company was part-way through the construction of a large house when the customer failed to pay an instalment of £70 000. As a result, the business could not afford to buy any more materials or pay the wages of its seven employees. Graham Parker, the managing director of GHP Contractors, was unable to raise any finance, so the company had to be wound up.

E

1 (a) A cash flow problem can result if cash outflows are greater than cash inflows.

Which of the following is an example of a cash inflow for GHP Contractors Ltd?   **(1 mark)**

Select **one** answer.

A ☐   Interest paid on a bank loan

B ☐   Wages paid to workers

C ☐   A customer payment for building a house extension

D ☐   Building materials bought using trade credit

(b) State **two** possible causes of cash flow problems.   **(2 marks)**

1 ....

2 ....

> Remember that explanations are not needed in this type of question.

B

2 (a) What is meant by the term '**productivity**'?   **(2 marks)**

....

....

....

Guided

(b) Describe **one** reason why productivity might decline in a business.   **(4 marks)**

Here is a plan you could use for your answer:
• Suggest a reason why productivity might fall – such as poor worker motivation or machinery that is out of date.
• Describe how productivity is likely to decline as a result.

....

....

....

....

....

....

....

Problems faced by the economy 1

In March 2012 the rate of inflation in the UK rose to 3.5% from 3.4% in February. It was the first rise in six months, after inflation peaked at 5.2% in September 2011. The Bank of England and the government had been hoping that inflation would keep falling this year, easing the financial burden on British households and businesses.

C

1 (a) Which of the following is used to measure the rate of inflation in the UK? **(1 mark)**

Select **one** answer.

A ☐ Gross domestic product

B ☐ Gross national product

C ☐ Consumer price index

D ☐ FTSE 100 index

(b) (i) State **two** possible causes of inflation. **(2 marks)**

1 ....

2 ....

> Remember that explanations are not needed in this type of question.

(ii) Explain how **one** of the causes identified in **(i)** might result in inflation. **(3 marks)**

....

....

....

....

> You need to explain how the cause you identified leads to price increases. You must include three **linked** sentences in your answer.

B

2 Describe how rising demand in the economy might affect a car manufacturer. **(3 marks)**

Guided

Here is a plan you could use for your answer:
• Define the level of demand in the economy.
• State how the level of demand in the economy can affect a business such as a car manufacturer.

....

....

....

....

Had a go ☐   Nearly there ☐   Nailed it! ☐

Problems faced by the economy 2

> In 2011, Ahmed Hussain – along with another 1700 people – was made redundant from his job at a large bank. He said: 'This is a miserable time for me and my family. There are no other jobs available where I live, because of government cuts and the global recession.'

D

Guided

1   (a)   Which of the following is used to measure unemployment in the UK?   **(1 mark)**

Select **one** answer.

A ☐   The number of people in long-term unemployment

B ☐   The number of people made redundant in a given month

~~C ☐   The consumer price index~~

D ☐   A monthly count of those people claiming unemployment benefit

> It isn't option C because the consumer price index is used to measure inflation.

(b)   What is meant by the term '**unemployment**'?   **(2 marks)**

....

....

(c)   State **three** costs of unemployment to the wider economy or society.   **(3 marks)**

1 ....

2 ....

3 ....

A

Guided

2   A global recession is an example of an external shock.

Discuss how UK businesses might be affected by an external shock.   **(6 marks)**

> Here is a plan you could use for your answer:
> - Outline what is meant by an external shock.
> - Give an example of a positive external shock.
> - Give an example of a negative external shock.
> - Suggest how each of the above might affect businesses.
> - Explain that the effect depends on whether the shock is positive or negative.

....

....

....

....

....

....

....

....

....

....

> Make sure your answer ends with a conclusion and contains and judgement.

Exchange rates 1

Britain has a long history of trading with overseas nations. Today, for example, Britain sells whisky to the US, seafood to Spain, cars to Italy and pharmaceuticals to India. Britain also buys machinery from Germany, wine from Australia, vegetables from Peru and clothes from Bangladesh.

D

1 (a) Which of the following is an example of an export for the UK? **(1 mark)**

Select **one** answer.

A ☐ The sale of cars to Italy

B ☐ The purchase of clothes from Bangladesh

C ☐ The transfer of £25 000 from a UK bank account to a US bank account

D ☐ A visit by a UK school party to France

Guided

EXAM ALERT

(b) What is meant by the term 'international trade'? **(2 marks)**

> Here is a plan you could use for your answer:
> • You need to mention imports and exports.
> • You could give examples.

> Students have struggled with exam questions similar to this – **be prepared!** ResultsPlus

....

....

....

A

2 In the first three months of 2012 the exchange rate between the pound and the euro changed from £1 = €1.18 to £1 = €1.22.

(a) What is meant by the term 'exchange rate'? **(2 marks)**

....

....

....

(b) Explain whether the pound has strengthened or weakened against the euro. **(4 marks)**

....

....

....

....

....

> Decide whether the pound can buy more or fewer euros.

Exchange rates 2

In early 2012, the exchange rate between the pound and the US dollar improved slightly.

B

1   Describe the impact that the strengthening of the pound might have on the prices of imports to the UK.   **(4 marks)**

....

....

....

....

> A strengthening pound benefits **importers**.

A

2   * Assess the effect of the strengthening of the pound against the US dollar on the profits of British whisky producers exporting to the US.   **(8 marks**

> **Guided**
>
> **EXAM ALERT**

Here is a plan you could use for your answer:
- Outline the effect on the prices of exports of the strengthening pound.
- Explain the effect on the US demand for whisky resulting from the effect on the prices of exports.
- Explain how the possible change in US demand will affect the profits of whisky producers.
- Suggest that the overall effect will depend on how much the pound has strengthened.

> Students have struggled with exam questions similar to this – **be prepared!** ResultsPlus
>
> Make sure your answer relates to British whisky producers.

....

....

....

....

....

....

....

....

....

....

....

....

....

The government 1

In recent years the UK government has tried to reduce the amount of money that the country owes. For example, it has made significant cuts in government expenditure. At the same time interest rates have been historically low, at 0.5%.

B

Guided

1 (a) Which of the following statements is **true** about interest rates? **(1 mark)**

Select **one** answer.

A ☐ Higher interest rates might cause unemployment

B ☐ Lower interest rates are likely to result in lower levels of inflation

C ☐ Interest rates might affect the demand for food

D ☐ The interest rate is set by the IMF

> It isn't option D because interest rates are set by the Bank of England.

(b) Explain how low interest rates will help stimulate demand in the economy. **(3 marks)**

....

....

....

....

> Consider how consumers and businesses might react to lower interest rates.

B

2 (a) State **two** aims of government expenditure. **(2 marks)**

1 ....

2 ....

Guided

(b) Explain how cuts in government spending might cause unemployment. **(3 marks)**

Here is a plan you could use for your answer:
- State the effect on the level of demand in the economy when government spending is cut.
- Explain the link between the level of demand and unemployment.

....

....

....

....

The government 2

The government can use fiscal policy to help resolve social problems and influence the level of demand in the economy.

B   1   (i)   State **two** social problems that the government might address.   **(2 marks)**

1 ....

2 ....

(ii)   Explain how **one** of the social problems you identified in (i) might be addressed using fiscal policy.   **(3 marks)**

....

....

....

....

....

> An 'Explain' question must have three **linked** sentences. Make sure you relate your answer to one of the social problems you identified in the first part of the question.

A   2   Two methods that the UK government might use to affect the level of demand are to:

> Guided

*   reduce government expenditure

*   raise taxation.

In your opinion, which of these two methods is more likely to **reduce** demand in the economy and why?   **(6 marks)**

> Here is a plan you could use for your answer:
> *   Explain how each method can affect demand in the economy.
> *   Discuss both methods, giving examples to support your answer.
> *   Make a judgement by saying which **you** think is the most effective.

....

....

....

....

....

....

....

....

....

....

> Remember there is no right or wrong answer but you must make a judgement about which method is more likely to reduce demand and **justify** your answer.

How businesses grow

In 2011, OilCorp, a large oil-processing company, merged with Kelham Oil, another oil-processing company. The chairman of OilCorp said: 'This merger will enable us to cut costs and give us a wider market share. There will be no redundancies and we look forward to the possibility of some takeovers in the future.'

(D) 1 (a) The merger described above is an example of: **(1 mark)**

Select **one** answer.

A ☐   forward vertical integration

B ☐   backward vertical integration

C ☐   horizontal integration

D ☐   a conglomerate merger

(b) Define the term '**takeover**'. **(2 marks)**

....

....

....

> A takeover might not be a voluntary transaction.

(C) 2 (a) Many businesses grow internally. What is meant by the term '**internal growth**'? **(3 marks)**

....

....

....

> **Guided**

(b) Describe how changing the marketing mix might help a business grow internally. **(4 marks)**

Here is a plan you could use for your answer:
• Choose one or more of the four Ps to talk about.
• Describe an example of how your choice above might result in growth.

....

....

....

....

....

....

Why businesses grow

Supermarkets such as Tesco, Asda and Sainsbury's are keen to grow because they can exploit economies of scale. In particular, they can buy goods from suppliers at much lower prices because they buy such large quantities.

B 1 **(a)** Which of the following best defines 'economies of scale'?   **(1 mark)**

Select **one** answer.

A ☐ A fall in total cost when businesses produce more

B ☐ Factors that result in falling average cost when output rises

C ☐ The way a business can dominate a market with lower average costs

D ☐ A rise in average cost when businesses produce too much

(b) State **three** other benefits of growth to a business (in addition to economies of scale).

(3 marks)

1 ....

2 ....

3 ....

> Remember that explanations are not needed in this type of question.

(c) (i) Identify **two** possible drawbacks of growth to a supermarket chain.   **(2 marks)**

1 ....

2 ....

> Think about the context of a supermarket chain.

Guided

(ii) Describe **one** of the drawbacks of growth identified in (i) to a supermarket chain.
(4 marks)

EXAM ALERT

> Here is a plan you could use for your answer:
> • Consider what might happen to average costs if the chain gets too big.

> Students have struggled with exam questions similar to this – **be prepared!** ResultsPlus

....

....

....

....

....

Monopoly power

Merseyrail operates a number of train services in Merseyside. It is the sole provider of rail services on most routes in the area. In 2012 there were some fare increases. For example, a return ticket from Manor Road (on the West Kirby line) to Liverpool increased by 4% from £3.80 to £3.95. More significantly, a single fare increased from £3.05 to £3.45, an increase of about 13%.

Source: adapted from www.wirralnews.co.uk

C

1 (a) The government defines a business as having monopoly power if it: **(1 mark)**

Select **one** answer.

A ☐ faces no competition in the market

B ☐ shares the market with just one other supplier

C ☐ has at least a 25% market share

D ☐ is a nationalised industry

(b) Merseyrail could be described as a natural monopoly. What is meant by the term **'natural monopoly'**? **(2 marks)**

....

....

....

B

2 (a) Explain how the owners of Merseyrail might benefit from its position as a monopolist. **(3 marks)**

....

Consider how much profit a monopolist might make.

....

....

Guided

(b) Explain one disadvantage to consumers of Merseyrail operating as a monopolist. **(3 marks)**

EXAM ALERT

Here is a plan you could use for your answer:
• Consider what might happen if prices are increased.

Students have struggled with exam questions similar to this – **be prepared!** ResultsPlus

....

....

....

....

An 'Explain' question must have three **linked** sentences. Make sure you relate your answer to Merseyrail.

Controlling big businesses

C

1 Identify **two** competition authorities used to control big businesses. **(2 marks)**

1 ....

2 ....

B

2 (a) Outline the role of pressure groups. **(2 marks)**

....

....

....

....

> Use key terms and accurate descriptions to support your answer.

(b) Describe the role of self-regulation in controlling businesses with monopoly power.

(4 marks)

....

....

....

....

A*

3 * Assess the extent to which self-regulation is an effective way to prevent big businesses from exploiting consumers. **(8 marks)**

Guided

> Here is a plan you could use for your answer:
> • Explain what is meant by self-regulation.
> • Discuss one or two advantages of self-regulation.
> • Discuss one or two disadvantages of self-regulation.
> • Explain that there might be better alternatives to self-regulation.
> • Make a judgement.

....

....

....

....

....

....

....

....

....

> Remember there is no wrong or right answer but you must make a judgement about how effective self-regulation is and **justify** your answer.

Growth

In recent years many European economies have struggled to grow. In some countries growth has been negative for a period of time. In 2012, growth in the UK was expected to be just 0.8%. Many have argued that the government should do more to help the economy grow.

B

Guided

1 (a) Which of the following is likely to help the economy grow? **(1 mark)**

Select **one** answer.

     A ☐   Higher levels of investment

     B ☐   Higher interest rates

     ~~C ☐   Higher taxation~~

     D ☐   Lower government expenditure

> It isn't option C because higher taxation is likely to reduce consumer spending.

     (b) Define 'economic growth'. **(2 marks)**

....

....

....

     (c) Explain how more government spending on education might help the economy to grow.

(3 marks)

....

....

....

....

> An 'Explain' question must have three **linked** sentences. Make sure you relate your answer to spending on education.

C

2 Describe how lower interest rates can help the economy to grow. **(4 marks)**

....

....

....

> Consider the effect of lower interest rates on business investment.

....

....

....

Growth and standard of living

According to a recent report, the UK is the worst place to live in Europe for quality of life, behind countries with damaged economies such as Ireland and Italy. The UK has the second-lowest number of hours of sunshine a year, the fourth-highest retirement age, and the third-lowest spend on health as a percentage of GDP. Also, despite higher incomes, Britons have 5.5 fewer days' holiday a year than the Europeans, and endure a lower government spend on education.

Source: www.guardian.co.uk

B 1 (a) The standard of living in a country can be measured using GDP per capita.

Which of the following best describes GDP per capita?   **(1 mark)**

Select **one** answer.

A ☐ The value of output produced by a country in a year multiplied by the population of that country

B ☐ The value of goods and services produced by a country in one year

C ☐ The value of all the money in the economy divided by the population

D ☐ The value of output produced by a country in a year divided by the population of that country

(b) State **two** possible problems with using GDP per capita to measure the standard of living.   **(2 marks)**

1 ....

2 ....

> Remember that explanations are not needed in this type of question.

A 2 (a) What is meant by the term '**quality of life**'?   **(2 marks)**

....

....

....

> Consider some of the factors mentioned in the case study.

Guided (b) Explain why the rate of life expectancy in a country might be an indication of its living standards.   **(3 marks)**

> Here is a plan you could use for your answer:
> • Define life expectancy.
> • Explain how an increase in life expectancy arises as a result of more income.

....

....

....

....

Can growth be bad?

> It is argued that one of the problems caused by economic growth is traffic congestion. This is because as a nation becomes wealthier, the number of cars purchased rises significantly. Congestion is expensive for the economy. It results in delays, wasted fuel, wasted time, extra wear and tear on vehicles, and driver frustration, which can cause accidents.

C

> Guided

1 (a) Congestion is an example of: **(1 mark)**

   Select **one** answer.

   A ☐ ~~a positive externality~~

   B ☐ a negative externality

   C ☐ resource depletion

   D ☐ a traffic-calming measure

   > It isn't option A because congestion is not a good thing.

   (b) State **two** ways in which congestion could be reduced.   **(3 marks)**

   1 ....

   2 ....

   (c) Another problem caused by fast economic growth is resource depletion.

   Describe what is meant by a '**non-renewable resource**'.

   ....

   ....

   ....

   > Support your answer with some examples of non-renewable resources.

C

2 Outline **one** way in which the government could reduce the consumption of non-renewable resources.   **(3 marks)**

   ....

   ....

   ....

   > You could consider the role of recycling.

Sustainable growth

Many governments are under pressure to promote growth that is sustainable. This involves increasing GDP without imposing costs on future generations, such as by using more renewable resources. Some businesses are helping by making more use of renewable resources and recycled materials.

D

> **Guided**

1 (a) Which of the following is a possible disadvantage to businesses of using renewable resources?   **(1 mark)**

   Select **one** answer.

   A ☐   Some renewable resources are not valuable

   B ☐   Legal barriers often prevent the use of renewable resources by business

   C ☐   The set-up costs of using renewable resources can be very high

   ~~D ☐   Using renewable resources might damage the image of the business~~

> It isn't option D because using renewable resources would help improve the image of a business.

(b) State **two** benefits to the wider economy of using more renewable resources.   **(2 marks)**

   1 ....

   2 ....

C

2 (a) What is meant by '**corporate social responsibility**'?   **(2 marks)**

   ....

   ....

   ....

> Think about the needs of a much wider group of stakeholders.

(b) State **three** reasons why businesses might behave more socially responsibly.   **(3 marks)**

   1 ....

   2 ....

   3 ....

> Remember that explanations are not needed in this type of question.

C

3 Some businesses are accused of 'greenwashing'.   **(2 marks)**

   What is meant by the term '**greenwashing**'?

   ....

   ....

   ....

Government action

HomeSun and ISIS Solar are examples of UK businesses benefiting from government subsidies given to households if they have solar panels fitted. Households get subsidies, which gives them cheap electricity and payment for any unused electricity that is fed back into the grid. Since the introduction of the subsidy in 2010 a huge number of businesses providing solar products have entered the market.

Ⓐ

1 **(a)** Which of the following best defines a 'subsidy'? **(1 mark)**

Select **one** answer.

A ☐ A payment to businesses or consumers to encourage the production of certain products

B ☐ A payment to businesses to help cover production costs

C ☐ A payment designed to increase the private cost of a business activity

D ☐ Money given to people on low incomes

〉Guided〉

(b) Describe the purpose of the subsidy provided in the case study. **(4 marks)**

> Here is a plan you could use for your answer:
> • Consider the effect on the environment of using solar power to generate electricity.

....

....

....

....

....

(c) Explain how businesses such as HomeSun and ISIS Solar will be affected by the subsidy provided. **(3 marks)**

....

....

....

....

> An 'Explain' question must have three **linked** sentences. Consider the effect on sales and profits for HomeSun and ISIS Solar.

Ⓓ

2 State **two** other ways in which the government can take action to protect the environment. **(2 marks)**

1 ....

....

2 ....

> Remember that explanations are not needed in this type of question.

....

Is everybody equal?

The population of Bangladesh is ten times that of Switzerland. The table below shows some of the key differences between the two countries in terms of income and welfare.

2011	Bangladesh	Switzerland
Population	76 million	7.6 million
GDP per capita	$1700	$43 400
Life expectancy	70 years	81 years
Literacy rate	47.90%	99.00%
Population below poverty line	31.50%	6.90%

Source: adapted from CIA World Factbook

B

1 (a) In Bangladesh 31.5% of the population lives below the poverty line.

What is meant by the term 'poverty line'? **(2 marks)**

....

....

....

> You need to give an accurate definition to get both marks. You could support your answer with an example.

(b) What is meant by the term 'absolute poverty'? **(2 marks)**

....

....

....

A

2 To what extent are living standards in Switzerland higher than in Bangladesh? **(6 marks)**

> **Guided**

Here is a plan you could use for your answer:
• Outline briefly what is meant by the terms listed in the table.
• Discuss living standards in Bangladesh.
• Discuss living standards in Switzerland.
• Explain which country has the better living standard.

....

....

....

....

....

....

....

....

....

> Remember that the standard of living refers to the amount of goods and services a person can buy with their income in a year. You must make a judgement about whether living standards in Switzerland are higher than in Bangladesh and **justify** your answer.

> Use the data in the table to support your answer.

International trade 1

Less economically developed countries (LEDCs) such as Kenya or Mozambique can benefit from international trade. For example, jobs might be created if an LEDC can export goods and services.

C

1 (a) Which of the following is a benefit of international trade to an LEDC?   **(1 mark)**

Select **one** answer.

A ☐ It lowers employment levels

B ☐ It raises the rate of interest

C ☐ It reduces GDP per capita

D ☐ It provides markets for commodities such as coconuts

(b) (i) State **three** possible costs of international trade to an LEDC.   **(3 marks)**

1 ....

2 ....

3 ....

(ii) Explain **one** of the costs to an LEDC mentioned in (i).   **(3 marks)**

....

....

....

Make sure you identify a cost and include two **linked** consequences of this cost.

A

2 Explain **one** way the Single European Market has improved living standards in the UK.   **(3 marks)**

....

....

....

....

Consider the range of goods and services consumers can now buy in the UK.

International trade 2

C   **1**   Which of the following is a possible motive for protectionism?   **(1 mark)**

Select **one** answer.

A   ☐   Tariffs

B   ☐   Protect infant industries

C   ☐   Decrease inflation

D   ☐   Increase investment from multinational corporations

B   **2**   Tariffs and quotas are two ways in which LEDCs can restrict free trade. Which **one** of these do you think is most likely to reduce imports to an LEDC and why?

Justify your answer.   **(6 marks)**

EXAM ALERT

> **Guided**

Here is a plan you could use for your answer:
- Explain how tariffs reduce imports.
- Explain how quotas reduce imports.
- State which approach you think is more effective. You could use an 'it depends' approach.

Students have struggled with exam questions similar to this – **be prepared!** ResultsPlus

....

....

....

....

.... | Remember there is no right or wrong answer, **but** you must **justify** for your answer.

....

....

B   **3**   **(i)**   State **two** benefits to an LEDC of multinationals setting up business operations in their country.   **(2 marks)**

1 ....

2 ....

(ii)   Explain **one** of the benefits you identified in **(i)** to an LEDC of multinationals setting up business operations in their country.   **(3 marks)**

.... | An 'Explain' question must have three **linked** sentences. Make sure you explain the benefit to the LEDC.

....

....

Other help for LEDCs

> In 2005, at a G8 meeting of finance ministers, an agreement was reached to write off the entire US$40 billion debt owed by 18 Highly Indebted Poor Countries to the World Bank, the International Monetary Fund and the African Development Fund. This helped many LEDCs. However, a lot still needs to be done to improve living standards in these countries.

B 1 (a) Which of the following organisations is **least** likely to give help to LEDCs? **(1 mark)**

   A ☐   The Confederation of British Industry (CBI)

   B ☐   Charities such as Oxfam and Christian Aid

   C ☐   The World Trade Organisation (WTO)

   D ☐   The Fairtrade Foundation

   (b) State **three** methods that a government might use to help LEDCs to develop. **(3 marks)**

   1 ....

   2 ....

   3 ....

   > Remember that explanations are not needed in this type of question.

   (c) Explain how **one** of the methods above would help an LEDC to develop. **(3 marks)**

Guided

   > Here is a plan you could use for your answer:
   > • You could consider how the debt burden of an LEDC could be reduced.
   > • You could discuss how an LEDC would benefit from reduced debt.

   > You need to include three **linked** strands that build the explanation with reference to the LEDCs.

   ....

   ....

   ....

B 2 Outline the role of the World Bank. **(3 marks)**

   ....

   ....

   ....

   > You could include an example in your answer.

   ....

Exam skills 1

On this page you can practise answering 1 to 3 mark questions.

In 2012 the government in the UK extended value added tax to include hot pastry products. The so-called 'pasty tax' was criticised by some businesses in the food industry. For example, Greggs, the high-street baker, blamed the tax for a decline in sales. In a statement, Greggs said that the government had made 'insufficient allowance for the Income Tax, NI contributions and Corporate Tax that would be lost, as well as the cost of extra unemployment pay, if stores were to close and workers lost their jobs'.

C

1   (a)   Which **one** of the following is a reason why the government raises taxes?   **(1 mark)**

    Select **one** answer.

    A ☐   To raise inflation

    B ☐   To raise demand in the economy

    C ☐   To reduce unemployment

    D ☐   To raise revenue to fund government expenditure

  (b)   (i)   Identify **two** Greggs' stakeholders that might be affected by the 'pasty tax'. **(2 marks)**

    1 ....

    ....

    2 ....

    ....

> Remember that explanations are not needed in this type of question.

   (ii)   Explain how **one** of the stakeholders in **(i)** might be affected by the 'pasty tax'.

                                          (3 marks)

....

....

....

....

....

B

2   The government often imposes taxes on goods that are price insensitive.

    Explain **one** benefit to a business if demand for its products is price insensitive.   **(3 marks)**

....

....

....

....

....

> Students have struggled with exam questions similar to this – **be prepared!** ResultsPlus

> If a product is price-insensitive there is scope for raising the price.

Exam skills 2

On this page you can practise answering 6 mark questions.

The supermarket industry is becoming increasingly competitive. However, in May 2012, one operator – Sainsbury's – said it enjoyed a good sales and profit performance in the year to 17 March, outperforming the market. Total sales were up 6.8% to £24.511 billion. Underlying profit before tax was up 7.1% to £712 million.

A

EXAM ALERT

1 Do you think that Sainsbury's would benefit from lowering its prices? Justify your answer.

(6 marks)

....

....

Students have struggled with exam questions similar to this – **be prepared!** ResultsPlus

....

....

Demand for the products sold by Sainsbury's are likely to be **price sensitive**.

....

....

....

....

....

....

A

Guided

2 Sainsbury's imports foodstuffs and other goods to sell in its stores. To what extent might the performance of the business be affected if the exchange rate strengthened?   **(6 marks)**

Here is a plan you could use for your answer:
- Define imports.
- Explain the impact of a strengthening exchange rate on imports.
- Explain the effect of cheaper imports for Sainsbury's.

....

....

....

....

....

For this type of question you must make a judgement about the **extent** to which the performance of the business is affected by strengthening exchange rates.

....

....

....

....

Exam skills 3

On this page you can practise answering 8 and 10 mark questions.

B

1 * High unemployment has many adverse affects, both on the individual and on the economy. Two measures to reduce unemployment include: **(8 marks)**

- reducing income tax
- lowering interest rates.

In your opinion, which of these two methods is likely to be more effective and why?

....

....

....

....

....

....

.... | For this type of question you must make a judgement about which of the two benefits is more important and **justify** your decision.

....

....

....

....

A*

2 * Using your knowledge of economics and business, assess the view that the benefits of economic growth outweigh the drawbacks.   **(10 marks)**

....

....

....

....

....

....

.... | For this type of question you must make a judgement about whether it is right or not that a business can satisfy all the needs of its stakeholders and **justify** your decision.

....

....

....

....

Practice exam paper – Unit 1

> *Edexcel publishes official Sample Assessment Material on its website. This practice exam paper has been written to help you practise what you have learned and may not be representative of a real exam paper.*

1 Which **one** of the following is a financial objective for a business?   **(1 mark)**

   Select **one** answer.

   A ☐ Higher profits

   B ☐ To help others

   C ☐ Provide customers with a good service

   D ☐ Independence

2 Which **one** of the following is a tax paid on the profit made by a private limited company in the UK?   **(1 mark)**

   Select **one** answer.

   A ☐ Value Added Tax

   B ☐ Income Tax

   C ☐ Corporation Tax

   D ☐ Capital Gains Tax

3 Which **two** of the following are **most likely** to be the qualities needed by an entrepreneur when running a business?   **(1 mark)**

   Select **two** answers.

   A ☐ A business qualification

   B ☐ The ability to make decisions using quantitative techniques

   C ☐ Initiative

   D ☐ An understanding of pensions

   E ☐ The power of persuasion

4 Which **one** of the following is an example of a cash outflow in a cash-flow forecast? **(1 mark)**

   Select **one** answer.

   A ☐ Sales revenue

   B ☐ Wages

   C ☐ Interest received on a bank deposit

   D ☐ A fresh injection of capital

Questions 5–8 are based on the passage below.

The Party Shop Ltd is run by Andrea and William Petrov. The business was set up in 2010 and sells fancy-dress costumes, party accessories, gifts and cards. They opened the shop because they thought there was a gap in the market in the town where they live. Andrea and William did some market research to assess the needs of potential customers in the local area. They interviewed about 300 people at a number of parties they attended in late 2009.

5 Andrea and William put £25000 of their own money into the business when it was set up. The **most** they could lose if the business fails is £25000. Why is this? **(1 mark)**

Select **one** answer.

This is because both owners have:

A ☐ unlimited liability

B ☐ no more money left

C ☐ limited liability

D ☐ personal liability

6 Which **two** of the following are **most likely** to add value to the business? **(2 marks)**

Select **two** answers.

A ☐ Extending opening hours on Friday and Saturday nights until 11.00 pm

B ☐ Merging with another party shop in a nearby town

C ☐ Buying costumes and accessories from local suppliers

D ☐ Providing a free delivery and collection service to customers

E ☐ Investing £5000 in a new advertising campaign

7 Andrea and William interviewed potential customers before opening the shop. This kind of research is called: **(1 mark)**

Select **one** answer.

A ☐ secondary research

B ☐ research and development

C ☐ primary research

D ☐ a market segment

8 In 2011 Andrea and William imported a consignment of costumes from Italy for €24000. The exchange rate at the time of the transaction was £1 = €1.20. How much did the costumes cost in sterling? **(1 mark)**

Select **one** answer.

A ☐ £1600

B ☐ £24000

C ☐ £28800

D ☐ £20000

Questions 9–14 are based on the information below.

> Felix Court Ltd manufactures high-quality home furnishings from natural materials for retailers in the south east. Unfortunately the market has been difficult in the last two years owing to the recession, and the company has had to lay off two of its six workers. The bar chart below shows some financial information for Felix Court Ltd in 2011.

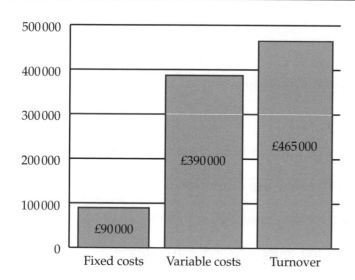

9 Which **two** conclusions can be drawn from the bar chart? **(2 marks)**

Select **two** answers.

A ☐ Total costs for 2011 were £480000

B ☐ Felix Court Ltd made a profit of £15000 in 2011

C ☐ Felix Court made a loss of £15000 in 2011

D ☐ Average costs were £2000 in 2011

E ☐ Prices in 2011 were too high

10 Which **one** of the following is an example of a downside for Felix Court Ltd? **(1 mark)**

Select **one** answer.

A ☐ Interest rates have been low for several years

B ☐ Staff turnover at Felix Court Ltd has been low for several years

C ☐ The recession resulted in lower demand for home furnishings

D ☐ Inflation looks set to fall in the future

11 Which **two** of the following are most likely to be examples of fixed costs for Felix Court Ltd? **(1 mark)**

Select **two** answers.

A ☐ Packaging

B ☐ Insurance

C ☐ Factory rent

D ☐ Factory wages

E ☐ Fabric

12 Which **one** of the following stakeholders is **most likely** to be affected by the financial information shown for Felix Court Ltd? **(1 mark)**

Select one answer.

A ☐ Government

B ☐ Customers

C ☐ Suppliers

D ☐ Shareholders

13 Which of the following is **most likely** to be a calculated risk for Felix Court Ltd? **(1 mark)**

Select **one** answer.

A ☐ Felix Court Ltd must lower prices by 15% to remain competitive

B ☐ Business costs have risen by more than 5% in the last 12 months

C ☐ The managing director of Felix Court Ltd reckons there is a 50% chance that the recession in the UK will continue until the beginning of 2013

D ☐ The cost of making two people redundant will reduce profit by about 10%

14 What is the **most likely** purpose of a business such as Felix Court Ltd? **(1 mark)**

Select **one** answer.

A ☐ To generate tax revenue for the government

B ☐ To provide goods and services to meet the needs of customers

C ☐ To provide community service

D ☐ To create jobs so that unemployment is not too high

Questions 15–19 are based on the information below.

Jenni has always owned animals and so have her friends. They have decided to offer an 'up-market' animal service so will charge a high price for their services. It will provide a range of grooming, sitting and walking services for different animals. They have drawn up a market map to assess the competition and decide if there is a gap in the market. They are also aware that some businesses offer franchise opportunities in pet care, animal-sitting services and food provision. Jenni knows the business will need a bank overdraft at first. It has been suggested that interest rates are forecast to rise in future.

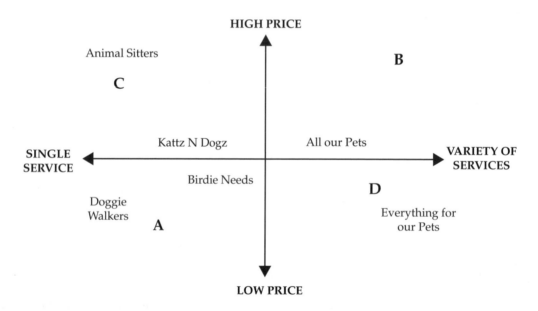

15 Where on the marketing map is the service provided by Jenni and her friends most likely to be in relation to competitors?

Select **one** answer. **(1 mark)**

A ☐

B ☐

C ☐

D ☐

16 Which **two** of the following are **most likely** to be of benefit to a franchisee when setting up in a franchise? **(2 marks)**

Select **two** answers.

A ☐ They will have freedom to make their own decisions

B ☐ There will be a fee that needs to be paid at the start

C ☐ They can be guaranteed to make a profit

D ☐ They can be trained in providing animal services

E ☐ There will be existing knowledge of the market

17 Which **two** of the following are **most likely** to give the business a competitive advantage over rivals? **(2 marks)**

Select **two** answers.

A ☐ Ensuring prices match those of competitors

B ☐ Providing a unique service

C ☐ Providing a service for the community

D ☐ Remaining open into the evening

E ☐ Taking out a bank loan

18 Which of the following is **most likely** to be an effect on the business of a rise in interest rates if it has an overdraft? **(1 mark)**

Select **one** answer.

A ☐ A deterioration in the cash flow of the business

B ☐ A reduction in the profit of the business

C ☐ An improvement in the outflows of the business

D ☐ An increase in the amount borrowed by the business

19 Which three of the following are **most likely** to help Jenni and her friends gain repeat business? **(3 marks)**

Select **three** answers.

A ☐ Employing three extra staff

B ☐ Coming out to people's houses to groom animals

C ☐ Offering a discount for prompt payment

D ☐ Buying soap powder from a cheaper supplier

E ☐ Increasing the number of animals they look after

F ☐ Gaining loyalty from customers

20 Match the definition on the left with the correct term on the right. Show your answers by drawing a line from the definition on the left to the matching term on the right. If you change your mind about the answer, cross out the line and draw a new line to mark your new answer.   **(5 marks)**

Definition	
The process of transforming ideas into products that can be brought to the market	i
Fluctuations in the level of economic activity over time	ii
The intentional creation of new ideas through recognised techniques	iii
The right of ownership of an invention or process when it is registered with the government	iv
The sum of money that flows into a business over time	v

Term	
A	Patent
B	Cumulative cash flow
C	Invention
D	Business cycle
E	Services
F	Innovation
G	Enterprise
H	Deliberate creativity

Practice exam paper – Unit 3

Edexcel publishes official Sample Assessment Material on its website. This practice exam paper has been written to help you practise what you have learned and may not be representative of a real exam paper.

Section A

Richer Sounds is a home cinema, television and audio equipment retailer. It has featured in the Guinness Book of Records for the highest sales per square foot of any retail outlet in the world. Richer Sounds values its employees. Holiday homes are provided rent-free for the use of all employees. There is personal contact allowed between all employees and senior managers.

1 (a) Providing holiday homes rent-free is **most likely** to be an example of: **(1 mark)**

Select **one** answer.

A ☐ salaries

B ☐ piece rates

C ☐ fringe benefits

D ☐ commission

(b) Identify **one** benefit of allowing contact between all employees and senior managers.

(1 mark)

....

(c) Explain **one** problem of allowing contact between all employees and senior managers.

(3 marks)

....

....

....

....

....

....

2 (a) Outline **one** method Richer Sounds could use to differentiate its services from other retailers. **(3 marks)**

....

....

....

....

....

....

(b) Explain **one** way in which differentiating the service can benefit the business.   **(3 marks)**

....

....

....

....

....

....

3   Richer Sounds includes a customer survey on all of its receipts.

(a) Identify **two** other methods of primary research that the business could use to
gather data.   **(2 marks)**

1 ....

2 ....

(b) Explain **one** way that carrying out primary research can benefit the business.   **(3 marks)**

....

....

....

....

....

Section B

The Mug Shot is a business that makes a variety of ceramic and pottery products. In 2012 the
UK was celebrating a number of important events and anniversaries, including the Queen's
Diamond Jubilee, the London 2012 Games, and 50 years after The Beatles released their first
single. The Mug Shot had decided to make some new products that reflected these dates.

The Mug Shot constructed
a break-even chart of one
of its new mugs to find
out the break-even point.
This is shown in Figure 1.

- It sells this mug for
  £10.
- Its fixed costs are £400.
- The variable costs of
  each mug are £5.

Figure 1

4 (a) What is meant by the term 'break-even point'? (1 mark)

....

(b) Using Figure 1, identify the number of mugs that The Mug Shot would need to sell to break even. (1 mark)

....

(c) Calculate the total profit or loss if the business sold only 40 mugs. (2 marks)

....

....

(d) The Mug Shot has decided to raise the selling price of its mugs. Explain **one** effect that this might have on the break-even chart of the business. (3 marks)

....

....

....

....

....

(e) Explain **one** disadvantage to The Mug Shot of raising its price. (3 marks)

....

....

....

....

....

5 The Mug Shot has always stressed the need for customer loyalty and good customer service.

(a) Which of the following is **most likely** to improve customer service?

Select **one** answer. (1 mark)

A ☐ Delaying payments to suppliers to improve cash flow

B ☐ Providing packaging that prevents mugs from breaking

C ☐ Replacing products only after proof of purchase is provided

D ☐ Replacing a full-time employee with a part-time employee

(b) Explain **one** advantage to the Mug Shot of developing customer loyalty. (3 marks)

....

....

....

....

....

6 The Mug Shot is considering how the new products will affect its stock control. It has decided to change to a Just-In-Time method of stock control for all its products.

(a) What is meant by the term 'Just-In-Time method of stock control'? **(2 marks)**

....

(b) * Assess the effect of the change to a Just-In-Time method of stock control for The Mug Shot. **(8 marks)**

....

....

....

....

....

....

....

....

....

....

Section C

Kleensoaps is a manufacturer of cleaning products. It promotes its products by stating that:

- it is an ethical and environmentally friendly business
- products are only sourced from ethical suppliers
- products are not tested on animals
- products are made using only natural ingredients
- suppliers are paid a fair price.

Kleensoaps must comply with UK and EU laws that affect its workers and how it advertises to the public.

7 Explain **one** benefit of complying with the legislation for Kleensoaps. **(3 marks)**

....

....

....

....

8 Other than advertising, explain **one** way in which Kleensoaps could change its marketing mix in order to improve its competitiveness. **(3 marks)**

....

....

....

....

9 Kleensoaps has recently found that one of its suppliers is engaging in unethical practices. It has decided to stop trading with that supplier. Identify **one** advantage and **one** disadvantage to Kleensoaps of following this action. For each, explain one likely effect on the business. **(8 marks)**

Advantage ....

Explanation ....

....

....

....

....

....

....

Disadvantage ....

Explanation ....

....

....

....

....

....

10 *Using your knowledge of business, assess whether all businesses should be environmentally friendly. **(10 marks)**

....

....

....

....

....

....

....

....

....

....

....

Practice exam paper – Unit 5

Edexcel publishes official Sample Assessment Material on its website. This practice exam paper has been written to help you practise what you have learned and may not be representative of a real exam paper.

Section A

It is argued that price cuts in video game systems often result in better sales. For example, a few years ago, a price decrease in the US in mid-October improved sales for the PlayStation 3 from 30 000 and 40 000 in weeks 1 and 2 to 75 000 and 100 000 in weeks 3 and 4, respectively. A further drop doubled sales again. After a price cut in Europe for the Xbox 360, sales more than doubled.

1 (a) Which of the following is true about lowering prices?   **(1 mark)**

Select **one** answer.

A price cut is likely to:

A ☐ reduce revenue if demand is price sensitive

B ☐ increase revenue if demand is price sensitive

C ☐ reduce costs if demand is price sensitive

D ☐ increase revenue if demand is price insensitive

(b) Explain **one** possible reason why price cuts in the video game industry result in better sales.   **(3 marks)**

....

....

....

....

2 Identify **two** stakeholders that might benefit from price cuts in the video game industry.

For each stakeholder explain how they will benefit.

Stakeholder 1 .... **(1 mark)**

Explanation ....

....

....

.... **(3 marks)**

Stakeholder 2 .... **(1 mark)**

Explanation ....

....

....

.... **(3 marks)**

3 Most businesses, once they get established, want to grow. **(1 mark)**

(a) Which of the following is a **not** a benefit of business growth?

Select **one** answer.

A ☐ Average costs might be lower owing to economies of scale

B ☐ Total costs might be lower owing to diseconomies of scale

C ☐ A firm might be able to dominate the market

D ☐ Higher revenue and profit

(b) Explain what is meant by '**external growth**'. **(3 marks)**

....

....

....

....

(c) Some firms grow very big and are able to enjoy monopoly power. To what extent is monopoly bad for consumers? **(6 marks)**

....

....

....

....

....

....

Since 2008 there has been a sharp increase in unemployment in many European countries, including the UK.

Unemployment rate in the UK

Source: www.tradingeconomics.com/united-kingdom/unemployment-rate

4 (a) Define the term 'unemployment'. **(2 marks)**

....

....

(b) State **two** costs of unemployment to the individual. (2 marks)

1 ....

2 ....

(c) Explain how lower levels of taxation in the economy might reduce unemployment. (3 marks)

....

....

....

....

5 Discuss how poor cash flow could lead to business failure. (6 marks)

....

....

....

....

....

....

....

Section B

Many countries in Europe – such as Spain, the UK, Greece and the Netherlands – experienced a recession in 2012. This means that economic growth was negative for two consecutive quarters. Many people in these countries were starting to see their living standards fall. It was argued by some that policies aimed at cutting government spending were contributing to the problem. Many government opponents were calling for measures to stimulate growth in the economy.

6 (a) What is meant by 'standard of living'? (2 marks)

....

....

(b) (i) State **two** ways in which the government might stimulate economic growth. (2 marks)

1 ....

2 ....

(ii) Explain how **one** of the methods identified in (i) will stimulate economic growth.

(3 marks)

....

....

....

....

(c) To what extent can economic growth be considered bad? (6 marks)

....

....

....

....

....

....

....

7 (a) What is meant by '**absolute poverty**'? (2 marks)

....

....

(b) State **two** ways in which a multinational company might help an LEDC. (2 marks)

1 ....

2 ....

(c) Describe the role that non-governmental organisations can play in reducing
international poverty. (4 marks)

....

....

....

....

....

....

Section C

Rolls Royce is the second largest manufacturer of aircraft engines in the world. It has many export markets. For example, in April 2012 the company signed a $598 million contract with the US Department of Defense for 268 AE 1107C engines for US Marine Corps and Air Force V-22 aircraft. Rolls Royce claims that the company is committed to helping the environment. For example, they invest nearly £900 million a year in research and development, two-thirds of which is aimed at improving the environmental performance of their products.

8 (a) Define the term 'export'.   (2 marks)

....

....

(b) Explain how a weakening pound would benefit Rolls Royce.   (3 marks)

....

....

....

....

....

....

(c) State **two** benefits to Rolls Royce of behaving responsibly.   (2 marks)

1 ....

2 ....

(d) Two measures a government can take to protect the environment are:

   • to encourage self-regulation

   • to impose legislation.

   Which of these two measures do you think is more effective and why?   (8 marks)

....

....

....

....

....

....

....

....

....

Answers

Unit 1

1. Businesses

1 B 2 D 3 A and D

2. Understanding customer needs 1

1 A, B and C 2 A

3. Understanding customer needs 2

1 D 2 B 3 C and D

4. Market mapping

1 C 2 A and E

5. Competition

1 C and E 2 B 3 A

6. Added value 1

1 B 2 D 3 D

7. Added value 2

1 B and E 2 D 3 C

8. Franchising 1

1 B 2 B 3 B and D

9. Franchising 2

1 A, E and F 2 A and B

10. Enterprise

1 C 2 A and C 3 A, E and F

11. Thinking creatively

1 C 2 B 3 B and D

12. Questions entrepreneurs ask

1 A and E 2 C 3 A

13. Invention and innovation

1 D 2 C 3 C and D

14. Taking a calculated risk

1 A 2 D 3 B and E

15. Other important enterprise skills

1 B 2 C and E 3 B

16. Objectives when starting up

1 B 2 B 3 A

17. Qualities shown by entrepreneurs

1 A, E and F 2 D 3 A

18. Revenues, costs and profits 1

1 B. Total costs = Variable costs of £600 (£3×200) + Fixed costs of £600 = £1200

2 C. Total revenue = Price (£12) × Quantity (200) = £2400

3 (a) £2200 (b) £200 (c) £2100
  (d) £2700

19. Revenues, costs and profits 2

1 A, D and F 2 B and D 3 D

20. Forecasting cash flows 1

1 A

2 C. Closing balance = Opening balance (£18 000) plus net cash flow (−£4000) = £14 000

3 (a) −£7000 (b) £14 000 (c) −£11 000

21. Forecasting cash flows 2

1 B and D 2 A and E 3 B and C

22. The business plan

1 B 2 C 3 i = E, ii = H, iii = A, iv = D, v = G

23. Obtaining finance 1

1 B, D and E 2 A 3 B and E

24. Obtaining finance 2

1 B 2 D 3 C

25. Customer focus

1 A and E 2 D and E 3 C

26. The marketing mix

1 A 2 D 3 C (product) and D (promotion)

27. Limited liability

1 D 2 C, D and F 3 A and C

28. Start-up legal and tax issues

1 D 2 A and B 3 B

29. Customer satisfaction

1 D 2 C and D 3 A and E

30. Recruiting, training and motivating

1 B and E 2 A and D 3 C

31. Market demand and supply

1 C 2 A, D and F 3 B and E

32. The impact of interest rates

1 B, D and E 2 A, C and F

33. Changes in exchange rates

1 B. It buys 200 models × $30 a month = $6000. This will cost $6000 ÷ 2 = £3000

2 A and D. A is correct because before the models cost £3000 and now they cost $6000 ÷ 1.5 = $4000. If costs rise and prices in the UK are the same, the profits fall on each sale, option D.

3 B

34. The business cycle

1 D and E 2 C

3 i = D, ii =H, iii = E, iv = C, v = A

35. Business decisions and stakeholders

1 A 2 B, C and F

3 i = G, ii = C, iii = H, iv = A, v = D

36. Exam skills 1

1 D 2 B 3 C

37. Exam skills 2

1 (a) £61 000 (b) £15 000 (c) £22 000
  (d) £37 000 (e) £12 000

2 A

3 i = G, ii = A, iii = E, iv = B, v = D

38. Exam skills 3

Below you will find a list which will help you to check how well you have answered the 'Choice' questions in Unit 6. The list shows a suggestion of points that you might have considered in your answer. A full answer will contain many of these points but does not have to include them all and may include other valid statements. Your actual answer should be written in complete sentences, contain relevant detail and link the points in a logical order.

1   Choice 1 – points to consider:
- bonuses or money is a great motivator
- depends on how much the bonus is
- they have security, they may not get another job even with higher pay
- they may work hard but not increase sales.

Choice 2 – points to consider:
- some workers are motivated by non-financial rewards
- it may increase loyalty to the business
- some workers may not like making decisions
- if decisions are taken by everyone it can be a problem for the business.

Unit 3

Below you will find the answers to all multiple choice questions and a list which will help you to check how well you have answered each written question. The list shows a suggestion of points that you might have considered in your answer and some examples of how these might have been written. Make sure you include the right number of points for the question; for example, an 'Identify' question may ask you to identify two points and an 'Explain' question will usually contain one point that is explained. A full answer for 6, 8 and 10 mark questions will contain many of these points but do not have to include them all and may include other valid statements. Your actual answer should be written in complete sentences, contain relevant detail and link the points in a logical order. Questions with an asterisk will also be awarded marks for the quality of written communication.

39. Marketing

1   (a)   B

(b)   Possible answers include:
- anticipating customer needs
- increasing sales and profits
- providing a better service
- making a profit.

Virgin Holidays will be marketing its flights and holidays effectively if it is anticipating and satisfying the needs of its customers accurately. Effective marketing leads to holidays that better meet the needs of customers. Because of this it should sell more and make more profit.

2   (a)   Possible answers include:
- age
- amount to spend on holiday/income
- departure airport/area of the country
- marital status
- children or not
- number in the group travelling
- type of holiday preferred (city or country; activity or relaxation)
- area of the world preferred
- star rating of hotel
- time of the year holiday taken.

(b)   Possible answers include:
- information from past bookings
- surveys
- questionnaires
- interviews by holiday reps at destinations
- information collected at travel agents.

Virgin Holidays might identify market segments by looking at past booking information. This could give Virgin Holidays information about the type of holidays customers book and when they took them. This will be accurate information as customers have actually taken these holidays and Virgin Holidays can use it to target customers effectively.

40. Market research

1   C

2   Qualitative research could give Tesco opinions about whether consumers find its products attractive or not. This might lead to Tesco changing parts of its marketing mix, such as its product design, to better suit consumer needs. As a result it will hope that consumers will buy more of its products.

3   (a)   Possible answers include:
- surveys
- questionnaires
- consumer panels
- focus groups
- observation

(b)   Possible answers include:
- costs involved
- targeting the right customers
- time taken to carry out research
- customers might not give their real opinions
- past figures might be outdated
- secondary data might be incorrect or biased.

(c)   If customers do not give their real opinions, the information collected will be inaccurate. If Tesco decides to change its marketing mix in response to this, then this could lead to the business making wrong decisions. As a result it might have higher costs or lower revenues than expected.

41. Product trial and repeat purchase

1   (a)   D

2   (a)   Repeat purchase is where customers return to buy a product they have previously bought, buying the product more than once.

(b)   Possible answers include:
- promotion
- reminder adverts
- setting a price that meets customers' expectations about value (low or high)
- offers such as BOGOF (buy one, get one free)
- product innovations and updates
- customer loyalty schemes (loyalty cards)
- making the products easily available in places customers want.

(c) Possible answers include:

- high cost of developing new products
- increasing sales
- expanding market
- competing effectively against rivals.

A food manufacturer might want to encourage customer loyalty and repeat purchases because it can often be difficult and expensive to attract new customers. Loyalty to a food product and repeat purchases lead to continued sales, as customers keep returning to buy the meal, drink or confectionery product. As a result, having repeat purchases can be cheaper for the food manufacturer and also ensure sales and success for a food product over the long term.

42. Product life cycle 1

1 (a) D

(b) Extension strategies are methods used by businesses to increase the life of a product, to prevent it falling into decline by maintaining its sales.

(c) (i) Possible answers include:

- promotional offers or discounts
- lowering prices
- improving the product
- advertising
- increasing the number of distribution outlets
- repositioning the brand
- changing the product in some way, e.g. introducing a new flavour or variety.

(ii) By introducing new flavours of the breakfast cereal – e.g. strawberry or peanut – the market for the cereal will be bigger. This means that it will be attractive to a larger number of people and so increase the likelihood of new sales.

43. Product life cycle 2

1 (a) C

(b) Possible answers include that it could help Devlin to:

- balance its product portfolio
- be able to see if it has too many of its products in one 'quadrant' of the Matrix
- identify which products to withdraw because they are 'Dogs'
- identify whether it has enough funds to support the marketing of 'Stars' or 'Problem children / Question marks'
- identify whether or not it will need to invest in innovation or R&D
- plan ahead.

The Boston Matrix puts products into categories or quadrants according to the growth rate and share of the market they have. This will help Devlin to see whether it has too many products in one category. For example, it might find that it has products other than Men's trainers in the 'Dogs' category and therefore needs to withdraw some of these products and introduce new ones, because they might lead to problems such as poor sales.

2 (a) The product portfolio is the range or combination of goods or services that a business sells to customers.

(b) Possible answers include:

- identify stages at which its products are at in their product life cycle
- know where its products are in the Boston Matrix
- know the levels of revenue generated by each product
- appreciate the need to advertise each product
- know if new products need to be developed or if products need to be discontinued
- identify costs savings.

Managing its product portfolio will help Devlin to identify which stages in the product life cycle its different sporting products are at. As a result it will know which products have sales that are rising and which have sales that are falling. Because of this it can make decisions about which products to take off the market and whether to introduce new products.

44. Branding and differentiation

1 (a) A brand is a named product that consumers see as being different from other products and which they can associate and identify with.

(b) Possible advantages include:

- consumers might be more willing to trial products in the brand range
- brands encourage consumer loyalty
- consumers trust brands, leading to repeat purchases
- brands can often charge premium prices
- consumers have greater awareness of brands.

One possible answer for an advantage:

Explanation: Customers loyal to the Apple brand are likely to make repeat purchases. This will lead to continued sales of goods, as consumers return to buy the same brand of mobile phone or computer when they upgrade or replace their products. As a result Apple should gain greater sales and profits over time.

Possible disadvantages include:

- customers who dislike one product in the brand range might not buy others
- higher-priced brands might put off some customers
- customers might feel non-branded goods are better value
- customers might feel put off by promotions associated with brands.

2 (a) Possible answers include:

- unique and catchy product name
- quality
- design, formulation or function
- packaging
- customer service
- differentiation across the value chain (at all stages in the production process).

(b) Possible answers include that it helps Apple to:
- position its products
- target different market segments
- gain an advantage over rivals
- show customers that their needs are being met better by its products than by other products.

Differentiating its products will help Apple's customers to see clearly how its computers or mobile phones are different from rival products. Because of this, customers can then compare products more easily and see how their needs are better met by Apple's products. As a result customers might develop loyalty to the product and sales might increase.

45. Successful marketing mix 1

1 (a) C

(b) Possible answers include:
- advertising (TV, magazines, radio, billboards)
- public relations
- word of mouth; viral or buzz marketing
- trade fairs or exhibitions
- product placement
- sales promotions/special offers (e.g. free samples)
- discounts (e.g. low introductory price).

Accept any three relevant answers. Watch out for awarding marks for points that are virtually identical, e.g. two methods of advertising.

(c) Possible answers include:
- part of an effective marketing mix
- ensure launch is effective
- increase consumer awareness
- reduce risk
- expand the market
- increase sales/profits.

Promotion is important to the success of the new game because people will not have heard of it or used it before. Promotion will make customers aware of the game and its features and, as a result, might encourage product trial. Playing is likely to sell more games the more people are aware of it and try it, so promotion leads to greater use and a greater chance of success for the new game.

2 Suggested answers include:
- easy comparison
- other factors affect choice
- effective competition
- ensure value for money
- influence consumer perceptions.

Charging a similar price to those of competitors will ensure that consumers do not see other products as cheaper or better value. Because of this they are likely to judge products on other features of the marketing mix. As a result PlayingZ's new game could be judged on function (the product element of the marketing mix) and, with its unique features, might prove more attractive and sell more.

46. Successful marketing mix 2

1 (i) A

(ii) If Next uses the right place to sell its products, it will make them more accessible to customers. As a result it is likely that there will be greater customer awareness, which could lead to increased sales for Next over time.

2 Answers might include the following arguments.

Reducing prices:
- increases size of the market
- will decrease revenue and profit per item
- could change perception of quality
- allows Next to out-compete rivals such as Top Shop, Dorothy Perkins, River Island, etc.
- can increase total revenue if sales increase is proportionately greater.

Advertising:
- increases the size of the market
- allows the business to target certain customers
- can add value
- increases customer loyalty
- allows Next to out-compete rivals such as Top Shop, Dorothy Perkins, River Island etc.
- can be expensive.

Suggested judgements include:
- Reducing prices is the better option because this might boost sales in the short term, but in the longer term increased advertising might be more appropriate, or some combination of price cuts and advertising.

OR
- Consider the drawbacks of reducing prices and/ or increasing advertising, as both would affect profit.

OR
- Use the 'it depends rule', where the solution might depend on the timescale, the nature of the market, the reactions of customers or the reactions of rivals.

47. Design and research development

1 (i) Possible answers include by:
- function   • cost   • appearance.

(ii) Possible answers include:
- how the product works differently to those from rivals
- how costs affect prices (lower or higher than those of rivals)
- how appearance can affect consumer perceptions of products against those of rivals.

The appearance of the product can influence consumer perceptions and buying. A Dyson bagless vacuum cleaner might appear more effective at cleaning than other products with bags. As a result, consumers might identify it more easily in promotions and develop a brand loyalty that other products do not have.

2 Possible answers include:
- a method of differentiating the product
- enhances the brand
- allows the business to stay ahead of competition
- allows the business to charge premium prices
- adds value
- develops new products.

Research and development is a way of adding value. This is because businesses will pay more for a hand drier that works efficiently. As a result their customers are likely to be more satisfied with their experience and return to a restaurant or public facility and there will be repeat business.

3 (a) A prototype is an early version or model of a product, which can be tested before it is then manufactured commercially.

   (b) Possible answers include:
   - improve design
   - reduce costs
   - prevent faults
   - reduce waste
   - get customer feedback.

   Creating a prototype will allow Dyson to test the product before it is produced and because of this it can prevent faults. As a result it can avoid costly mistakes, faulty products and returned products. These could all damage Dyson's reputation and harm sales and profits.

48. Managing stock 1

1 (a) C   (b) 20 models   (c) 2 weeks

   Stock arrival date (6 weeks) – Reorder date (4 weeks) = 2 weeks.

   OR

   Stock arrival date (10 weeks) – Reorder date (8 weeks) = 2 weeks.

   OR

   Stock is ordered in week 4 and arrives in week 6. Therefore 6 – 4 = 2 weeks.

   (d) Suggested answers include:
   - businesses can meet unpredicted surges in demand
   - businesses can replace damaged goods
   - a business can receive discounts for bulk buying
   - limits problems with deliveries from suppliers.

   Holding stocks can help the business to cope with surges in demand for models at certain times of the year, such as Christmas. The business will have enough stock to meet demand and will not run out. Without this stock of models it could potentially lose sales.

49. Managing stock 2

1 (a) Just-in-time method of stock control is a stock management system where stocks are delivered only when they are needed by the production system and so no stocks are held in the business.

   (b) Possible advantages include:
   - lower levels of stock
   - higher profit
   - lower costs
   - storage facilities not required
   - excellent relationships with suppliers can help overcome problems more easily.

Possible disadvantages include:
- increased risk
- not being able to meet demand
- damage to a brand
- cannot respond to changes in the market
- requires excellent relationships with suppliers, which are not easy to maintain

One possible answer for a disadvantage: Not being able to meet demand.

Explanation: If Mintchell's runs out of stock it might not be able to provide cycle shops when they require them. This means that it will not have cycles to sell to its customers and might order from other manufacturers. Because of this Mintchell's might find that it does not get repeat orders and that sales fall.

50. Managing quality

1 (a) Quality is the minimum standard of product or process, which must be achieved in producing or providing a good or service that meets customers' needs.

   (b) Possible answers include:
   - improved reputation
   - brand indentification
   - increased sales
   - more competitive
   - increased profit
   - customer loyalty
   - repeat purchases.

   Because Panasonic has quality products it is likely to get a good reputation. This will encourage repeat purchases by customers who develop brand loyalty. As a result it is likely to take sales from other brands.

2 (a) D

   (b) Answers might consider the following arguments.

   Quality control:
   - managers put controls in place and can control the business
   - workers might not feel part of the quality system
   - workers might feel it is a criticism of them
   - a lot of wastage
   - many systems flawed
   - can be cheaper
   - can be less time-consuming.

   Culture of quality assurance:
   - embraces all staff
   - improves motivation
   - improves satisfaction
   - good for reputation
   - prevents costly mistakes being made before final production
   - takes time to establish a business culture
   - training and reorganisation implications
   - can be expensive and time-consuming.

   Possible judgements:
   - A culture of quality assurance is the better option because although setting up a culture of quality assurance can be expensive in the

short term, because of the training required, in the long term the benefits of better motivation, faults being prevented before they occur and improved reputation will mean returns outweigh the costs.

OR

- Use the 'it depends rule', where the solution might depend on the type of business, the market or the resources available.

51. Cost-effective operations and competitiveness

1 (a) Possible answers include:
- improved purchasing (cheaper suppliers)
- better design of products
- cheaper labour costs
- cutting overhead costs
- streamline the production process
- relocation.

(b) Possible answers include:
- lower prices
- increased advertising
- investment in new equipment
- expanding product range
- improved products/designs
- retrain/hire labour
- spending on R&D compared to rivals.

Compartmentals might be able to lower the prices of its products to consumers because its costs have fallen. If its furniture prices are lower, then customers are more likely to buy its products than those of rivals. Compartmentals should see sales of its furniture increase as a result.

(c) Answers might consider the following ideas.

Setting competitive prices:
- attracts customers
- increases profit
- gives value for money
- allows easy comparisons with rivals
- encourages repeat purchases.

Improved productivity:
- lowers unit costs
- raises output
- increases profit
- increases efficiency.

Possible judgements:

Compartmentals might gain competitiveness by reducing prices but it depends on the reactions of rivals, because they might also reduce their prices and, if so, improved productivity is a better strategy.

OR

The answer might argue that the time period is important, e.g. 'A cut in prices might give a short-term boost to sales, but the business might lose profit over time by continuing with this strategy and so increasing productivity is the better option.'

52. Effective customer service

1 (a) B

(b) Possible answers include:
- meet and exceed needs of customers
- provide quality services, e.g. improve taxis or improve timekeeping
- innovation (keep moving forward)
- spot problems and potential problems and solve them
- listen to customers and make changes to the service in response
- deal effectively and quickly with complaints
- train staff better.

2 Possible areas to be considered in the answer include:
- the added value of an improved service
- the costs of an improved service
- any reorganisation or staff training that might be needed to give the improved service
- the levels of sales that could be achieved by good service
- the effect on efficiency of an improved service
- the opportunity for repeat purchases that an improved service brings
- the ability to develop brand loyalty to the taxi firm
- the opportunity that improved service gives to set competitive prices
- the chance to show consumers that an improved service gives value for money.

Suggested judgements:

Improved customer service adds to quality levels, thus giving an increased opportunity for the business to move ahead of its rivals. The increased sales that could result are more than likely to offset the costs of the improved service and in the long term it should be more profitable for the business.

OR

Use the 'it depends' rule, where whether or not an improved service allows the business to gain a competitive advantage over rivals will depend on issues such as the extent to which prices can be lowered, consumers' views, whether rivals also make improvements, or whether brand loyalty is possible in this area or service.

53. Consumer protection laws

1 The Sale of Goods Act or the Trade Descriptions Act.

2 The answer might consider the following factors:
- whether there is anything that legally prevents the use of terms such as 'natural ingredients'
- whether the facts are correct or not or whether any of the phrases are misleading
- whether the quiche matches the description and is fit for purpose for people looking to lose weight
- whether it is ethical to imply that it is more suitable than other products for those aiming to lose weight
- whether the business has to pay a fine if it breaks the law

- whether consumers feel that the information is misleading and their spending habits change as a result

- whether information is being withheld.

Mixon might be contravening the Trade Descriptions Act if it is ruled by law that its information about the weight-loss properties of its products is misleading. It could be breaking the Sale of Goods Act if its quiche does not match the description given in its advertising. It could be fined, but also the reputation of the business could be affected and sales could fall.

On the other hand, if all the information in the advertising is correct about the product then it might not be breaking any law. Also, the language used might be common in advertisements for such products and so consumers might not find them misleading. Consumers can also compare information on fat contents with those of other products.

In conclusion it could be argued that as long as any possible fine does not affect its reputation or harm the brand too much, e.g. reducing sales, then it is right to advertise its products using these phrases as they are likely to attract customers who feel the product is meeting their needs.

54. Improving cash flow

1 (a) D

(b) Possible answers include:
- to keep up loan repayments
- to keep the machinery
- to cope with late payments by customers
- to prevent a lack of confidence from customers
- to allow materials to be ordered given reduced inflows.

Without strong cash flow the business might not be able to keep up payments on its machinery. If the business defaults on the payments it might have to pay charges from the bank or higher interest payments. This will reduce its profits.

2 Possible advantages include:
- immediate boost to cash flow
- can use money for other purposes
- does not have to find other sources of inflows
- can delay payment period.

One possible answer for an advantage: Delay payment period

Explanation: If the payment period is delayed Jayston Printing might be in a better position to make payment. It might have other money coming in from other sources, or lower outflows, e.g. its own customers might have made their payments by this time. So it will be in a better position to pay the invoice without causing cash-flow problems, which could affect its ability to pay its loan.

Possible disadvantages include:
- reputation for late payment
- adverse effect on relationship with suppliers
- possible higher costs as a result of late payment
- need to find the money at a later date.

55. Improving profit

1 (a) B

(b) Profit is the financial reward to a business that results when its revenues are greater than its costs over a period of time.

2 Possible answers include:
- lower motivation
- high staff turnover
- reduced productivity
- affect reputation
- not enough staff to meet demand.

Reduced labour costs could lead to high staff turnover. If staff at Primark stores leave and are not replaced, then stores might not be able to deal with customers effectively. As a result customers might shop at other clothing stores, such as Next or New Look.

3 Possible answers include:
- advertising
- changing price
- adding value
- branding
- improving customer service
- improving quality of the product
- boosting revenue/sales/demand.

A business could increase advertising. This could lead to greater awareness and interest of customers in Primark's products and, because of this, the business should earn more revenue through increased sales. As long as revenue increases more than costs, then profits should increase.

56. Break-even charts

1 (a) D   (b) 16 sessions.

(c) £10 000.

(d) Profit = total revenue – total cost.
If 24 sessions are sold £12 000 – £10 000 = £2000

57. Break-even analysis

1 (a) Break even = fixed costs ÷ contribution per unit

New selling price = £570. Fixed costs = £4000. Variable costs = £250 per session

Contribution = selling price (£570) – variable cost (£250) = £320

Break even = £4000 ÷ 320

Therefore break even = 12.5 sessions

(b) Possible answers include:
- understanding if decisions in the past were correct or not
- setting and achieving production targets
- help when launching a new product
- help when expanding a business
- as part of a business plan.

Launching a new product is risky and knowing the break-even point can help reduce the risk. If Yffects decided to expand into hiring PA equipment, knowing the output/sales needed to break even would help the business to decide whether to go ahead or not. It could make decisions about whether the price was high enough or costs were low enough to make a profit.

2 **(a)** A

(b) Possible answers include:

- shows the business how many sessions it needs to sell to break even
- shows the business how many sessions it needs to make a profit
- allows the business to gauge how far demand can fall before it makes a loss
- allows a business to decide if it has the capacity to develop new products using the profit made
- use the information to persuade banks to lend money
- use the data to assess whether sales targets are realistic.

The margin of safety allows the business to gauge how far demand can fall before it makes a loss. As a result it can plan for unanticipated changes in demand and assess whether a product can still make a profit even if sales are lower, or whether changes in price or costs need to be made as sales fall to continue to be profitable.

58. Financing growth

1 **(a)** C

(b) Possible answers include:

- no interest to be paid
- does not involve issuing new shares so percentage ownership of existing shareholders is not diluted
- easier and quicker to proceed
- shows how much is available
- no loans to be applied for
- not being in debt.

(c) Using retained profit means that it is easier to proceed with plans. The money is already within the business and, as a result, Pret a Manger will know exactly how much it has available and can move ahead quickly. Because of this it is in a better position to expand at the right time and this is more likely to result in success.

2 Possible disadvantages include:

- interest could be charged, which could fluctuate, increasing or decreasing costs and affecting planning
- need to repay the loan with interest, which could affect cash flow and liquidity
- risk of failure if the loan is not repaid in time
- the need for collateral
- the bank might not be willing to lend.

Borrowing from a bank means that a business has to pay interest. This will increase the fixed costs of borrowing to the business, reducing profit.

59. Organisational structure

1 **(a)** B

(b) A hierarchy in a business is the structure of different levels of authority in the organisation, one on top of the other.

(c) Possible answers include:

- to empower workers
- to motivate workers
- to spread the workload
- to take the pressure off superiors
- to improve efficiency
- to give work to those best suited to it.

2 Possible advantages include:

- better control
- common decisions
- standardisation/consistency in decision making
- better vision for the business.

Possible disadvantages include:

- slower decisions
- loss of flexibility
- decision are not taken by those who are in the best position to take them
- demotivating for workers.

One possible answer for a disadvantage: Demotivating for workers.

Explanation: Workers and managers at the five sites might become demotivated, as the ability they previously had to make decisions is taken away. They might be less productive or flexible and some could leave as a result. Because of this the costs of Chisel Newton could rise and its output could fall, leading to reduced profit.

60. Motivation theory

1 **(a)** Motivation is the drive and desire to complete a task or to achieve something.
In the workplace, motivation is closely linked to the performance and productivity of the workforce.

(b) C

(c) Suggested answers could include:

- greater bonuses
- respect from superiors
- chance to express yourself in your work
- job security
- friendships with work colleagues.

2 Possible benefits include:

- better productivity
- better quality of service
- improved staff retention
- better sales
- better customer experience
- higher profits
- improved creativity.

Possible drawbacks include:

- costs of motivation
- time-consuming
- staff might resist
- finding the right methods/culture.

Possible judgements:

- Consider whether benefits outweigh costs.

OR

- Use the 'it depends' rule taking into account the aim of the business, the degree of competition or the time period.

61. Communication

1 (i) Suggested answers include:
- too many people
- too many messages
- jargon
- skills of sender or receiver
- feelings or behaviour of sender or receiver
- faulty or unsuitable equipment.

(ii) Using terms that are jargon can make communications difficult to understand. If the receiver does not understand the terms for different ingredients, they could misinterpret messages. As a result they might not order the correct ingredients, which might lead to lower-quality products and therefore loss of sales.

2 Answers might consider the following:
- improves product quality
- increases worker motivation
- prevents excessive communication
- ensures correct instructions are given and received
- increases flexibility
- increases profit
- increases productivity
- lowers units costs.

Possible judgements:

- Discuss which element is the most important, for instance in the case of the The CrustCake Bakery it could be argued that ensuring there is not so much information that instructions are ignored is the most important, as this has resulted in deliveries not arriving and a loss of customers.

OR

- Use the 'it depends' rule, considering the advantages of better communication against the possible drawbacks, such as the costs of making improvements or changes to the business that might be needed, which could affect customers' views.

OR

- Use the 'it depends' rule to consider whether the goal of communication is more important than other goals, such as maintaining the brand name, improving cash flow, or offering lower prices.

62. Remuneration

1 (a) A

(b) Possible answers include:
- commission
- wages
- fringe benefits
- payment by results
- piece rates
- shares in the company.

(c) Suggested answers include:
- improved motivation
- staff retention
- better service
- increased sales
- rewards related to effort
- increased profit
- better customer service
- reputation of business benefits.

If permanent staff are paid a bonus they are more likely to be motivated. They might work harder and be more efficient in order to make sure that the tutoring service is good and the website works well, because this will lead to more customers and profits, and their bonus is linked to profit.

(d) Suggested answers include:
- lower quality
- work might be slow to make more money
- reward not related to effort or quality
- does not encourage loyalty to business
- can lead to delays.

Workers who are paid by the hour might work slowly in order to increase the total payments they receive. This could lead to delays in work being done for the website, which could reduce the quality of its service and harm its reputation in the eyes of customers.

63. Ethics in business

1 Possible answers include:
- higher costs
- decreased profits
- consumers not willing to pay more for higher-priced products
- cannot compete on price with other products
- not enough consumers value ethical products
- target market not large enough.

2 (i) Possible answers include:
- add value
- source of product differentiation
- gives USP
- focus on market segment
- improved reputation and consumer loyalty
- established brand
- motivated workers.

(ii) By taking an ethical stance Cafédirect will have a clear USP and because of this consumers can see clearly how the products are different from those of rivals. As a result consumers might value Cafédirect's products more highly and this is likely to lead to consumer loyalty, repeat purchases and increased sales in future from those consumers.

3 (a) Possible answers include:
- boycott
- adverse publicity
- campaign/advertising
- website/blog
- direct action
- lobbying of government.

(b) Possible answers include:
- damage to brand
- increased costs
- reorganisation

- change in production/packaging/ingredients
- lost revenue
- loss of market share.

A pressure-group campaign could lead the bread manufacturer to change its ingredients. It might have to move to more costly ingredients as a result and this could lead to its having to increase its price or face reduced profit.

64. Environmental issues

1 **(i)** Possible answers include:
- recycling
- biodegradable/reusable or reduced packaging
- using environmentally friendly materials
- reduction in travel/low-emission travel
- working with suppliers who are environmentally friendly
- use of renewable energy
- replenishment and conservation of natural resources
- investing in machinery that pollutes less.

(ii) If UKOS used recycled paper for its paper products it would buy less paper. As a result fewer trees would need to be cut down and because of this there would be less chance of problems such as deforestation and less need for costly replanting.

2 Benefits could include:
- makes government regulation less likely
- enhances the brand
- will allow more market segments to be targeted
- gives UKOS a USP
- adds value
- allows premium pricing in some cases
- increases profits.

Drawbacks could include:
- increases costs
- could lower profits
- customers might care but are more interested in prices charged
- reorganisation and retraining of staff required
- could reduce efficiency if suppliers are used that are less efficient but more environmentally friendly.

Possible judgements:
- Consider whether benefits ourweigh costs.

OR

- Use the 'it depends' rule taking into account the views of the business, its customers and the hire period.

65. Economic issues affecting international trade

1 **(a)** B

(b) A tariff is a tax put on a product imported into a country which makes a the product more expensive for buyers in that country.

(c) **(i)** Possible answers include:
- quotas
- incomes/income distribution in these countries
- growth rates in these countries
- trading restrictions
- subsidies given to businesses in these countries.

(ii) If growth rates in India and China increase, the people are likely to have more money. Because of this the markets might be expanding and demand for exports might increase. As a result UK businesses can sell more products into India and China and make more profit.

66. Government and the EU

1 **(i)** Possible answers include:
- Value Added Tax (VAT)
- Corporation tax
- National Insurance contributions (NI)
- Income tax.

(ii) VAT is a tax on luxury items that makes certain products more expensive for consumers. This might mean that consumers spend less on items with VAT as they get less for their money. Because of fewer sales, business profits might fall.

2 Answers might consider the following factors.

In favour of the increase:
- reduces exploitation and motivates workers
- not ethical to allow wages to fall below a certain level
- increase is not great so costs are not really affected
- will make work more attractive to unemployed
- could increase spending in the local area
- helps workers faced with inflation.

Not in favour of the increase:
- might increase unemployment
- employers might expect workers to do more work rather than hiring extra workers
- increases employers' costs
- increases the chances of business relocating to other countries with a lower (or no) minimum wage
- disincentive to businesses to hire workers
- businesses might cut costs elsewhere to pay for wages affecting R&D, investment, etc.

Possible judgements:
- Consider whether benefits outweight the costs.

OR

- Use the 'it depends' rule taking into account the impact on workers, the ecomomy, consumers, businesses or the hire period.

67. Exam skills 1

1 D

2 Possible answers:
- mistakes/errors
- delays
- increased costs
- poor motivation
- poor productivity.

3 The amount of stock held by a business at which an order for new stock is placed with suppliers.

4 Possible answers include:
- adds value
- gives competitive advantage
- develops customer loyalty
- allows premium prices to be charged
- leads to repeat business
- enhances the brand.

5 Possible answers include:
- product differentiation
- adds value
- finds new products
- allows premium prices to be charged
- enhances brand
- gives competitive advantage.

68. Exam skills 2

1 Points to consider:

Reducing prices:
- lower sales revenue per item
- demand might not increase
- revenue might or might not rise, depending on price sensitivity
- other factors than price might be affecting sales
- relatively easy to cut prices
- makes business more competitive
- increases customer loyalty.

Cutting costs:
- reducing stocks/supplies can affect sales
- difficulty in cutting costs without affecting the business
- what costs to cut
- might not be possible to cut some costs, i.e. interest payments
- might be a better long-term strategy as reduces waste, i.e. flowers that don't sell
- how suppliers might react to cuts in supplies
- how customers might react to cuts in costs, i.e. shorter opening hours.

Conclusion:
- Consider the benefits against the costs of each method.

OR
- It depends on factors such as the reactions of customers, suppliers, rivals or the time period.

2 Points to consider:
- some workers motivated by factors other than pay
- some workers might not like extra responsibility or decision making associated with non-financial rewards
- pay, a financial reward, is often a major factor affecting motivation
- might depend on other factors such as the real value pay rise.

Conclusion:

It depends on factors such as the type of worker, timescale, type of reward, size of reward or existing pay.

A discuss question means a judgement must be made about the importance of non-financial rewards.

69. Exam skills 3

1 Possible benefits include:
- attract customers
- increased sales
- increased profits
- good reputation
- repeat business and customer loyalty
- attract employees
- gain a competitive advantage over rivals.

An 'assess' question means that a judgement must be made on which benefit is most important, or the extent to which the advantages of operating as an ethical business outweigh the disadvantages, such as increased costs.

2 Points to consider:
- different stakeholders often have conflicting interests
- similar groups of stakeholders have similar interests
- conflicts might be related to particular issues
- stakeholders have similar interests at particular times.

Conclusion:

It depends on nature of need being satisfied, nature of conflict or the time period.

This question ask for a judgement to be made about whether it is possible to satisfy the needs of all of its stakeholders.

Unit 5

Below you will find the answers to all multiple choice questions and a list which will help you to check how well you have answered each written question. The list shows a suggestion of points that you might have considered in your answer and some examples of how these might have been written. Make sure you include the right number of points for the question; for example, an 'Identify' question may ask you to identify two points and an 'Explain' question will usually contain one point that is explained. A full answer for 6, 8 and 10 mark questions will contain many of these points but do not have to include them all and may include other valid statements. Your actual answer should be written in complete sentences, contain relevant detail and link the points in a logical order. Questions with an asterisk will also be awarded marks for the quality of written communication.

70. Trade-offs

1 (a) C

(b) Trade-offs occur when the selection of one choice results in the loss of others. In this case, if Welham Park Council spends the £5 million on providing 100 new homes, it will lose the benefits from two other possible projects. The two trade-offs will be the conversion of a disused warehouse into a new, multi-purpose community centre, and the repairing of potholes and upgrading of local roads. The benefits from these other two projects will be sacrificed for the new homes.

(c)   The opportunity cost of providing 100 new council homes is the benefit lost from the next best alternative. According to the list of preferences, the next best alternative is the conversion of a warehouse into a community centre. As this alternative has been forgone, so have the benefits that could have been enjoyed.

71. Raising and lowering prices

1   (a)   A

(b)   Possible answers include:

- the high number of restaurants in Southport
- the ease with which customers can switch between restaurants
- restaurant meals are not necessities.

For example: There are lots of restaurants in Southport so competition is very fierce. This means that if a particular restaurant raises its prices customers can easily find cheaper alternatives. Therefore, demand for restaurant services in Southport is price sensitive. There will be a significant change in demand when a particular restaurant changes its price.

(c)   North West Water is a monopolist in the supply of water in the Southport area. This means that all water-users in the area have to buy their water from North West Water. Consequently, the demand for water will be price insensitive. If North West Water raises the price of water there will be very little change in demand because customers cannot switch to another supplier.

72. Stakeholders

1   (a)   A

(b)   Possible answers include:

- employees
- managers
- customers
- government
- local community.

(c)   (i)   Possible conflicts include:

- employees and owners (shareholders)
- employees and managers
- employees and customers
- managers or owners and customers.

(ii)   Shareholders are most interested in the profit made by BHP Billiton and the dividends that they receive. The first conflict outlined in (c) is having an impact on production. It states that supplies to customers might be affected. This might mean that orders and sales will be lower as a result of the strike. This is likely to lead to lower revenues and lower profits.

Therefore, shareholders might suffer lower profits and lower dividend payments. Also, in the long run, if the strike is not settled quickly, customers might find alternative suppliers. This could have an impact on the long-term profitability of BHP Billiton.

73. Hidden costs or benefits

1   (a)   D

(b)   Possible answers include:

- job creation
- more choice for consumers
- the nine extra homes for the local community
- extra business for the local community.

2   Explain that the development of the New Metro Supermarket can affect third parties – i.e. those outside the business.

Explain the effects of two possible negative externalities, such as congestion and failure to meet the council's targets for sustainability (e.g. construction and renewable energy standards).

Explain the effects of two possible positive externalities, such as job creation or the attraction of more business to the area.

Decide whether you think planning permission should be given and justify your answer. For example; you think it should go ahead because new jobs would be valuable in a climate where unemployment is rising nationally.

74. Measuring success

1   (a)   B

(b)   Possible answers include:

- profit
- market share
- revenue
- the level of corporate socialresponsibility.

(c)   Possible answers include:

- profits increased
- evidence of social responsibility.

For example: One important measure of business success is the amount of profit made. In 2011 the profit made by M&S rose to £598.6m – up from £523m in 2010. This is a lot of money and also shows an increase of around 10%. Most people would agree that this improvement suggests that the business has been successful in 2011.

2   Possible answers include:

- meeting the needs of employees
- meeting the needs of the local community
- taking into account the firm's environmental impact
- meeting the needs of customers
- adopting an ethical stance.

For example: social success is the performance of a business which takes into account the social environment and ethical factors. For example, M & S has donated money, food, equipment and clothes to charities, reduced some energy costs by 25%, adopted a 5-year plan to stop sending waste to landfill sites and adopted a 5-year plan to encourage healthier eating. These actions are ways in which a business can improve social success.

75. Causes of business failure

1   (a)   C

(b) Possible answers include:

- bad debts
- an unexpected fall in demand
- allowing too much credit
- seasonal demand
- poor cash management
- unexpected expenditure.

2 (a) Productivity is the output per worker or machine over a period of time. For example, output per worker can be calculated if total output is divided by the number of workers.

(b) Possible answers include:

- poorly motivated workers
- inadequate training
- poor management
- out-of-date machinery
- lack of flexibility.

For example: A decline in productivity could result if workers are poorly motivated. For example, output might fall if workers are unhappy with the working conditions. Poor working conditions, such as a working environment that is too hot and lacking in fresh air, might result in workers slowing their pace of work or taking unscheduled breaks. This might cause a fall in total output and therefore reduce productivity.

76. Problems faced by the economy 1

1 (a) C

(b) (i) Possible answers include:

- rising demand
- rising costs
- rising commodity prices
- higher fuel cost
- lower interest rates.

(ii) If demand rises too quickly, so that demand is outpacing supply in the economy, prices are likely to rise. There might not be enough goods being produced for the rising level of demand. As a result prices are driven up, causing inflation.

2 The level of demand refers to the spending that takes place in the economy. It might come from consumers, businesses, foreigners or the government. When the level of demand rises, businesses will usually benefit. For example, if there is more consumer demand, a car manufacturer might sell more cars and decide to increase production. This might result in higher profits.

77. Problems faced by the economy 2

1 (a) D

(b) Unemployment is when people who want to find work cannot do so.

(c) Possible answers include:

- higher state benefits
- lower output
- increased crime
- less social interaction
- less enterprise
- decline in standards of behaviour.

2 State that an external shock is an event that is beyond the control of the government.

Example of a positive event for exporters might be a fall in the exchange rate.

Example of a negative event might be a global recession.

A fall in exchange rates is good for exporters.

A global recession is bad for most businesses because the level of demand is likely to fall.

Generally, there are likely to be more negative external shocks than positive.

78. Exchange rates 1

1 (a) A

(b) International trade involves the buying and selling of goods and services between different countries. Exports are goods sold by the UK to other countries, such as the sale of pharmaceuticals to India. Imports are goods bought by the UK from other countries, such as vegetables from Peru.

2 (a) Exchange rate is the value of one currency in terms of another. For example, at the beginning of 2012 the exchange rate between the pound and the euro was £1 = €1.18.

(b) Over the time period it has moved from £1 = €1.18 to £1 = €1.22. This means that the pound has got stronger. This is because the £1 can buy more euros now compared with at the beginning of the year. One pound can buy an extra €0.04 or 4 cents.

79. Exchange rates 2

1 The exchange rate is the rate at which one currency exchanges against that of another. When the pound gets stronger it means that a pound can buy more of another currency. This will have an impact on the prices of exports and imports. The price of imports will fall when the pound gets stronger. This makes imports cheaper.

2 When the pound gets stronger, the prices of exports get higher.

If export prices are higher, then the price of whisky to US buyers will also be higher. As a result the demand for whisky is likely to fall.

A fall in demand for whisky means that sales revenue is likely to fall, which is also likely to result in lower profits for whisky producers.

The extent of the effect will depend on how much stronger the pound becomes. If the pound gets very strong, then the reduction in profits will be greater.

80. The government 1

1 (a) A

(b) Low interest rates will stimulate demand in the economy because borrowing will be encouraged. For example, businesses might borrow more to invest and consumers borrow more to buy consumer durables. This means that there will be an increase in the level of demand in the economy.

2 (a) Possible answers include:

- provide essential government services
- regulate demand in the economy
- resolve social issues like child poverty.

(b) Government spending is an important part of total demand in the economy. Therefore, a cut in government spending will reduce total demand. This means that businesses will not have to produce as much, so they will lay off workers. This will raise unemployment.

81. The government 2

1 **(i)** Possible answers include:
- binge drinking
- smoking
- congestion
- truancy
- anti-social behaviour
- child poverty.

(ii) (Binge drinking) Higher taxes on alcohol are likely to increase the price of alcohol in outlets. This should help to reduce demand for alcohol, which in turn should reduce consumption. Lower consumption might reduce the ill effects of drinking too much.

2 Demand in the economy can be affected by levels of government expenditure because government spending is an important component of total demand.

Taxation can affect levels of demand in the economy because it can have an impact on the amount of income consumers have to spend, for example.

The government could reduce spending by cutting the number of police officers employed. This would reduce demand because there would be fewer people employed with a reasonable level of disposable income.

The government could raise income tax, which would reduce demand in the economy. This is because workers and the self-employed would have less disposable income.

I would suggest that cutting government expenditure would be the best way because tax increases are more direct and might 'hurt more'. Also, people might compensate for the cut in disposable income by spending their savings or borrowing more.

82. How businesses grow

1 **(a)** C

(b) A takeover occurs when one business buys another business. The owners can agree to the sale of a business to another but if a business buys enough shares in another, it is able to take control.

2 **(a)** Internal growth occurs without the involvement of another business. Internal growth is also called organic growth and means that a business increases size by selling more of its output in current and new markets.

(b) Internal growth occurs without the involvement of another business. A business might grow internally by changing its marketing mix. For example, a business might decide to invest in a new promotion campaign. It might design a new advertising campaign to raise awareness of a product and encourage more sales. The campaign might draw in new customers and persuade others to be loyal to the product.

83. Why businesses grow

1 **(a)** B

(b) Possible answers include:
- higher revenue
- higher profit
- survival
- spread risk
- greater market domination.

(c) **(i)** Possible answers include:
- diseconomies of scale
- inflexibility
- loss of focus.

(ii) If a supermarket chain gets too big it might suffer from diseconomies of scale. This means that average costs will start to rise after a certain point. This could result in the supermarket becoming less competitive and possibly losing market share to its rivals. This could also reduce profitability. Rising costs could result from coordination and communication difficulties with a chain that is too large.

84. Monopoly power

1 **(a)** C

(b) A natural monopoly exists if costs are lower when only one firm supplies a product or service. In this case, Merseyrail is the only provider of certain rail services in Merseyside.

2 **(a)** The owners of Merseyrail are likely to get higher profits. This is because monopolists do not face any competition. Therefore they can raise their prices and enjoy more revenue and profit.

(b) Consumers can be exploited by monopolists. For example, a monopolist might raise prices because there is no competition. In this case, one of the fares charged by Merseyrail has gone up by 13%! Customers who want to travel in Merseyside by train have no choice but to use Merseyrail services. They are forced to pay the higher prices.

85. Controlling big businesses

1 Possible answers include:
- The Competition Commission (CC)
- The Office of Fair Trading
- Specialist regulators for specific industries, such as Ofwat for water regulation
- The EU Competition Commission.

2 **(a)** Pressure groups aim to influence the decisions of business, government and individuals. They unite individuals so that they have more power acting as one group. They use tactics such as boycotts, protests, marches and advertising to raise their profile.

(b) Self-regulation is where an industry monitors its own actions so it can take responsibility for making sure it is acting in the public interest. Companies are responsible for following a list of guidelines and good practice that is drawn up, and face government intervention if they do not follow them.

3 Self-regulation is where an industry monitors its own actions.

Self-regulation is cheap because it avoids the need for legislation or controlling bodies. Also, it will work because firms will fear government intervention.

Self-regulation might be ineffective because there is too much self-interest. If a firm does not have very much competition there is no incentive to be efficient.

Regulatory bodies are more likely to prevent consumer exploitation because they have the backing of the law and can penalise businesses.

I think self-regulation is ineffective because there are too many examples of consumer exploitation in our society.

86. Growth

1 (a) A

(b) The amount of goods and services produced in the UK is called the gross domestic product (GDP). Economic growth is the percentage increase in GDP over a period of time – usually measured over one year.

(c) If people are better educated they will be more productive. This means they will be capable of producing more. Therefore, if the government invests in education, people will have improved skills and can produce more. This will help the economy to grow.

2 Interest is the cost of borrowing money, usually from a bank. Lower interest rates can encourage businesses to invest. This is because a good proportion of business investment is funded by borrowing, and borrowing costs are lower if interest rates are lower. Also, consumers might borrow more and spend more. This will create more demand in the economy and businesses should respond by producing more output. This would help the economy to grow as well.

87. Growth and standard of living

1 (a) D

(b) GDP might be understated, because not all output is counted.

GDP is an average and assumes everyone earns the same, whereas in reality some earn more but many less.

If the population is small, GDP rates can give an inaccurate picture.

2 (a) The quality of life is an individual's overall sense of well-being. This measure includes a range of factors in addition to the amount of goods and services that can be bought. An example might be the amount spent on health and education.

(b) Life expectancy is the number of years for which a person is expected to live in a particular country. Clearly, if people are able to live longer this suggests that living standards are better. This is because people generally live longer if they have enough good-quality food, enough clothes, adequate shelter, good health care and a hygienic living environment.

88. Can growth be bad?

1 (a) B

(b) Possible answers include:

- road charging
- higher vehicle duty
- higher fuel tax

- encourage car sharing
- encourage greater use of public transport
- improve traffic management or increase capacity.

(c) A non-renewable resource is a resource that is limited in supply. They will eventually run out completely and future generations will have to go without. Examples include oil, gas, coal, iron ore and diamonds.

2 One way the government could reduce resource consumption is to encourage recycling. It could do this by encouraging consumers to recycle waste such as paper, clothes, glass and other refuse. The provision of collection services would achieve this. It might also encourage businesses to make more use of recycled materials.

89. Sustainable growth

1 (a) C

(b) Possible answers include:

- less pollution, i.e. by using wind power instead of fossil fuels to generate electricity
- future generations will have more non-renewable resources to use
- it might be cheaper in the long run.

2 (a) Some businesses take measures to reduce the impact their activities have on society and the environment. They attempt to meet the needs of a wider group of stakeholders. This is called corporate social responsibility.

(b) Possible answers include:

- to avoid breaking the law
- to attract ethical investors
- improve their image and raise sales
- because of media and public pressure.

3 Greenwashing is when a business tries to give the impression that they are environmentally friendly – in their advertising, for example. However, in reality they are actually not genuinely behaving in that way.

90. Government action

1 (a) A

(b) The feed-in-tariff subsidy is designed to encourage households to install solar panels to generate electricity. Producing electricity using solar panels will help to reduce carbon emissions. This is because less power will be generated from the burning of fossil fuels, which creates high levels of carbon emissions.

(c) Businesses such as HomeSun and ISIS Solar will benefit from the feed-in-tariff subsidy. This is because they will sell more of their solar products, such as the installation of solar panels. Higher sales should result in higher revenues and higher profits.

2 Possible answers include:

- taxation
- legislation
- advertising/publicity campaigns.

91. Is everybody equal?

1 (a) The poverty line is the extent to which people in a country live in poverty – for example, the

number of families living on less than a certain amount of money per week.

(b) Absolute poverty is when people are unable to afford the basics of life such as food, shelter and clothes.

2 The table contains a list of indicators that reflect living standards. For example, GDP per capita shows the amount of income each citizen receives on average. The literacy rate is the proportion of people who can read in the country.

Indicators suggest that Bangladesh has a very poor standard of living. For example, GDP per capita is only $1700.

In Switzerland living standards appear very high. For example, GDP per capita is $43 400.

All of the indicators in the table suggest that Switzerland has a much higher standard of living than Bangladesh.

92. International trade 1

1 **(a)** D

(b) **(i)** Possible answers include:
- increased foreign competition
- higher unemployment
- overspecialisation
- lower tax receipts
- threat to domestic industries.

(ii) If LEDCs start trading with other nations this will increase the volume of imports. These imports could provide fierce competition for domestic producers. If domestic producers cannot compete with foreign goods they might go out of business, which would raise unemployment.

2 One of the benefits to the UK of belonging to the Single European Market is that the volume and range of imports increases. This means that there will be more choice for UK consumers. For example, the range of foods available in the UK has increased with the arrival of European cuisine. This extra choice helps to raise living standards.

93. International trade 2

1 B

2 A tariff is a tax on an import which makes it more expensive. Therefore, demand for imported goods is likely to fall because they are dearer.

A quota is a physical limit on the amount that is allowed into a country.

I think quotas are the best method because although tariffs make imports dearer, consumers still might buy them. Quotas are a forced restriction.

It could depend on the price sensitivity of imports. For example, if demand for a certain imported good is price insensitive, tariffs might be ineffective.

3 **(i)** Possible answers include:
- multinationals create jobs for locals
- multinationals will pay tax to the government of an LEDC
- they might increase exports for the LEDC
- they might develop the infrastructure in an LEDC.

(ii) Multinationals create jobs for locals by building factories and other businesses. Local people then have more money to spend in their local economy and this creates a multiplier effect, which benefits other businesses and the economy of the LEDC.

94. Other help for LEDCs

1 **(a)** A

(b) Possible answers include:
- cancel debt
- encourage free trade
- give financial aid
- increase investment in LEDCs
- encourage diversification.

(c) A government could help a LEDC to develop by cancelling debt. This means the LEDC would not have to repay loans and interest. As a result the government of the LEDC would be able to keep more of the tax receipts. The extra money could be spent on education, for example, which would help the country develop and reduce poverty.

2 The main aim of the World Bank is to reduce world poverty. It can do this by giving financial help such as low-interest loans, interest-free credit, and grants to LEDCs. For example, the bank might provide cheap loans for capital projects such as irrigation in LEDCs.

95. Exam skills 1

1 **(a)** D

(b) **(i)** Possible answers include:
- employees
- shareholders
- customers
- the government.

(ii) Greggs say that the 'pasty tax' has resulted in a decline in sales. If the decline in sales is significant it could lead to shop closures. This means that some workers would lose their jobs. As a result they could have to rely on state benefits, which would reduce their living standards.

2 If demand for a product is price insensitive it means that a change in price will not result in a significant change in demand. This means a business can raise its prices without suffering a large drop in demand. As a result revenue and profits are likely to rise.

96. Exam skills 2

1
- Explain that the supermarket industry is very competitive, with many strong rivals.
- Explain that demand for the products sold by Sainsbury's is likely to be price sensitive owing to the competitive market.
- Explain that if prices are lowered demand will rise along with sales revenue and hopefully profit. Therefore, Sainsbury's will benefit.

2
- State that imports are goods bought from overseas.
- Explain that the prices of imports are affected by the exchange rate.
- Explain that a strengthening exchange rate means that imports become cheaper.
- Explain that cheaper imports might result in lower costs and higher profits for Sainsbury's.

97. Exam skills 3

1
- Define unemployment.
- Explain that lower income tax will raise disposable incomes and result in higher levels of demand. This should encourage firms to produce more and take on more workers.
- Explain that lower interest rates reduce the cost of borrowing.
- If borrowing is cheaper businesses might invest more and consumers might borrow more to buy consumer durables, for example.
- Make a judgement. It doesn't matter which measure you think is better. However, you must justify your choice. For example, you might say that lower interest rates are better because they help businesses and consumers.

2
- Define economic growth.
- Discuss the benefits of growth, such as improved living standards, increased government tax revenue that can be spent on public services, more choice and better-quality products.
- Discuss the drawbacks of growth such as resource depletion, waste, pollution, inflation and stress.
- Make a judgement. It doesn't matter which measure you think is better. For example, you might argue that if growth is sustainable, then the benefits should help to outweigh the drawbacks.

98 Unit 1 – Practice exam paper answers

1	A	2	C	3	C and E
4	B	5	C	6	A and D
7	C	8	D	9	A and C
10	C	11	B and C	12	D
13	C	14	B	15	B
16	D and E	17	B and D	18	A

19 B, C and F

20 i = F, ii = D, iii = H, iv = A, v = B

105 Unit 3 – Practice exam paper answers

Below you will find the answers to all multiple choice questions and a list which will help you to check how well you have answered each written question. The list shows a suggestion of points that you might have considered in your answer and some examples of how these might have been written. Make sure you include the right number of points for the question; for example, an 'Identify' question may ask you to identify two points and an 'Explain' question will usually contain one point that is explained. A full answer for 6, 8 and 10 mark questions will contain many of these points but do not have to include them all and may include other valid statements. Your actual answer should be written in complete sentences, contain relevant detail and link the points in a logical order. Questions with an asterisk will also be awarded marks for the quality of written communication.

SECTION A

1 (a) C

   (b) Possible answers include:
   - Better motivation
   - Staff feeling as if they matter
   - Belonging/self-esteem needs satisfied
   - Staff retention
   - Reduced labour turnover.

   (c) Possible answers include:
   - Excessive communication
   - Senior staff overburdened
   - Delays in communication
   - Organisation of communication process
   - Costs and time involved.

2 Possible answers include:

   (a)
   - Cheaper prices
   - Catering for customers' needs (i.e. listening rooms)
   - Better information about products
   - Brand name
   - Better after-sales service.

   (b)
   - Repeat purchase
   - Customer loyalty
   - Increased sales
   - More profit
   - More competitive against rivals
   - Added value.

3 Possible answers include:

   (a)
   - Questionnaires
   - Street survey
   - Postal survey
   - Observation
   - Online request for information
   - Customer groups.

   (b)
   - Better able to meet customer needs
   - Identify problems
   - Target customers
   - Market segmentation
   - More sales and profits.

SECTION B

4 (a) Where the total revenue earned by the business from production and sales is equal to the total costs of that level of output.

   (b) 80 mugs.

   (c) If 40 mugs are sold total revenue = £400, total costs = £600, so there is a loss of £200 as costs are higher than revenue.

   (d) Possible answers include:
   - Increased total revenue at all output
   - Reduction in the level of output needed to break even
   - Increased profit above the break-even point
   - Reduced loss below the break-even point
   - Increase in the margin of safety at output above the break-even point.

   (e)
   - Reduced sales
   - Less competitive
   - Loss of customer loyalty
   - Loss of repeat purchase
   - May change brand image.

131

5 (a) B

(b) Possible answers include:
- Repeat purchases
- Strong brand
- Attracts new customers
- Guarantees sales
- Word-of-mouth advertising.

6 Possible answers include:

(a) A production method where stocks are delivered only when they are needed in the production process and so no stocks are kept.

(b) Points to consider:

Advantages:
- storage facilities not needed
- reduced cost
- quicker process
- less damage to stocks and less wastage
- more competitive pricing.

Problems:
- requires good relationships with suppliers
- possible delays in production
- lose out on discounts for bulk buying
- inability to meet surges in demand
- might not have stock to replace damaged goods.

Conclusion:

Could depend on:
- the time frame – sales are needed at the time of these anniversaries
- whether advantages outweigh disadvantages for this business.

SECTION C

7 Possible answers include:
- Avoid fines
- Customer loyalty
- Good public image
- Good reputation among employees
- Low staff turnover
- Motivated staff.

8 Possible answers include:
- Place – change the places in which the products are available to the public (shops, online)
- Product – change the ingredients, design style, packaging
- Promotion – use forms of promotion other than advertising (viral marketing, online, discounts, sales, PR)
- Price – change the price to customers so that they get better value or see it as a premium product.

9 Possible answers include:

Advantages:
- can comply with its ethical stance
- attractive to customers
- reinforces brand
- may find cheaper suppliers
- public reputation enhanced.

Disadvantages:
- may lose so supply
- alternative may be more expensive

- other suppliers may be affected
- delays in deliveries due to reorganisation.

Conclusion:

May depend on:
- how quickly/whether new suppliers can be found
- whether costs outweigh benefits.

10 Possible answers include:

Problems of being environmentally friendly:
- higher costs
- restricted suppliers
- limited market
- promotional restrictions
- reorganisation needed.

Benefits of being environmentally friendly:
- attracts customers
- builds brand
- enhances reputation
- motivational for staff.

Conclusion:

May depend on:
- type of business
- views of stakeholders
- whether they can still make a profit or not.

110 Unit 5 – Practice exam paper answers

SECTION A

1 (a) B

(b) Possible answers include:

Price cuts in the video games industry are likely to result in better sales because demand is price sensitive. This means that demand is responsive to price changes, i.e. demand will change significantly when there is a change in price. The main reason for this is probably because there is a lot of competition in the market.

2 Possible answers include:

(a) Stakeholder 1: Consumers

Consumers will benefit from price cuts in the video games industry because they will be able to buy games at a lower price. This means that they can buy more of the product or they will have money left over that they can spend on other products. Consumers will feel better off.

Stakeholder 2: Employees

Employees will benefit from price cuts because sales will increase. As a result production levels will need to be raised. This means that there will be more work and might lead to higher wages being paid. For example, existing workers might be able to work overtime and earn more money.

3 (a) B

(b) External growth means that a business expands by joining forces with another business. This could involve a merger or a takeover. When two or more firms join together, growth occurs very quickly.

(c) Possible answers include:

Monopoly might be bad for consumers because when one firm dominates the market consumers might be exploited. For example, prices might be higher and there might be a lack of choice.

On the other hand there might be benefits to consumers of monopoly. For example, because of their size, monopolists can be in a better position to exploit economies of scale. This means that costs can be lower, with the possibility of lower prices. Also, large monopolists can be more inclined to invest in research and development and bring out new products.

The extent to which monopoly is bad for consumers might depend on the effectiveness of government controls. For example, if the government exerts very little control over monopolies, consumers are more likely to be exploited.

4 (a) Unemployment exists when people who want to find work are unable to do so.

   (b) Possible answers include:

   Lower incomes, falling living standards, stress or depression, family tensions, loss of skills or health problems.

   (c) If income tax is cut then workers will have more disposable income. This means that they can spend more, which drives up demand. Firms might respond to the increase in demand by producing more. This is likely to result in more workers being employed.

5 Possible answers include:

   • Cash is the lifeblood of business. Without cash a business cannot survive.
   • If a business runs out of cash it might not be able to pay workers or suppliers.
   • If a business cannot pay workers they are not likely to work and therefore the business cannot operate.
   • Also, if a business cannot pay suppliers they are not likely to supply any more materials and therefore the business cannot operate.
   • It is vitally important for a business to make sure it has enough cash to meet its payments at all times.

SECTION B

6 (a) The standard of living refers to the amount of goods and services a person can buy with their income in a year. If a person has more income, they can buy more goods. This means their standard of living has improved.

   (b) (i) Possible answers include:

      Encourage business investment by lowering interest rates, invest in the infrastructure, invest in education and training, encourage more consumption.

      (ii) If the government lowers the interest rate, businesses might be encouraged to borrow more money to invest. This is because borrowing is cheaper and the returns on investment will then be higher. They might expand their businesses or buy new machinery and equipment.

   (c) Possible answers include:

      (i) Encourage business investment by lowering interest rates, invest in the infrastructure, invest in education and training, encourage more consumption.

      (ii) If the government lowers the interest rate, businesses might be encouraged to borrow more money to invest. This is because borrowing is cheaper and the returns on investment will then be higher. They might expand their businesses or buy new machinery and equipment.

7 (a) Absolute poverty exists when people are unable to afford the basics of life, such as food, water, shelter and clothes.

   (b) Possible answers include:

   Provide employment, encourage enterprise, pay tax to the LEDC and increase exports.

   (c) Examples of non-governmental organisations include the World Bank, the World Trade Organisation (WTO), the Fairtrade Foundation and charities such as Oxfam. They can help LEDCs in different ways. For example, the World Bank provides cheap finance for LEDCs, which can be used on capital projects such as irrigation. The WTO aims to promote free trade by encouraging nations to remove trade barriers. Charities such as Oxfam and Christian Aid collect donations and give money directly to people in LEDCs.

SECTION C

8 (a) Exports are goods and services that are sold to overseas customers. An example is the aircraft engines that Rolls Royce are selling to the US Defence Department.

   (b) Possible answers include:

   A change in the exchange rate will have an impact on the prices of exports and imports. If the pound gets weaker the price of exports will fall. This will help Rolls Royce because it means that the engines they sell abroad will be cheaper for their foreign customers. This would probably result in an increase in demand from overseas buyers.

   (c) Image will improve, avoid breaking the law, attract ethical investors and ethical consumers, there will be less media and public pressure.

   (d) Self-regulation is a 'soft' approach to controlling businesses. It means that firms will monitor their own actions.

   Firms might set up codes of practice or issue industry guidelines.

   Self-regulation is cheap for the government.

   Legislation, such as waste legislation, is a much tougher approach to controlling businesses. It involves passing laws that businesses must obey.

   For example, legislation might restrict the amount of emissions a business is allowed to release into the atmosphere.

   Fines and other penalties can be used if the law is broken.

   Legislation is probably the most effective because there are penalties if the law is broken.

   However, it can depend on how much a business has to lose. Bad publicity can often have harmful affects if self-regulation fails to work.

Published by Pearson Education Limited, Edinburgh Gate, Harlow, Essex, CM20 2JE.

www.pearsonschoolsandfecolleges.co.uk

Copies of official specifications for all Edexcel qualifications may be found on the Edexcel website: www.edexcel.com

Text and original illustrations © Pearson Education Limited 2012
Edited and produced by Wearset, Boldon, Tyne and Wear
Illustrated and typeset by HL Studios, Witney, Oxfordshire
Cover illustration by Miriam Sturdee

The rights of Dave Gray and Rob Jones to be identified as authors of this work have been asserted by them in accordance with the Copyright, Designs and Patents Act 1988.

First published 2012

16 15 14
10 9 8 7 6 5

British Library Cataloguing in Publication Data
A catalogue record for this book is available from the British Library

ISBN 978 1 446 90376 6

Printed in Slovakia by Neografia

Acknowledgements
Every effort has been made to contact copyright holders of material reproduced in this book. Any omissions will be rectified in subsequent printings if notice is given to the publishers.

In the writing of this book, no Edexcel examiners authored sections relevant to examination papers for which they have responsibility.